MAKE YOUR RESUME TALK

Richard A. Hart

There is no magic in writing an effective resume. It requires planning and effort, but the results of a well-written, targeted resume that talks for you will be worth the effort. Start now, accept the challenge, and build a resume that will get you interviews.

I want you to be able to start writing or re-writing your resume immediately. Therefore, the Background on the Book and Layout, Testimonials, Why I Wrote This Book, Author's Resume, and Acknowledgements that are usually in the front are shown in the Appendix. Now, let's get started so we can get an interview. There are places marked "TAKE ACTION." Those places are where you need to write sections to build your resume.

© Copyright 2006 Richard A. Hart
All rights reserved. No part of this publication may be reproduced, stored in a retrieval system, or transmitted, in any form or by any means, electronic, mechanical, photocopying, recording, or otherwise, without the written prior permission of the author.

Note for Librarians: A cataloguing record for this book is available from Library and Archives Canada at www.collectionscanada.ca/amicus/index-e.html
ISBN 1-4120-6828-2

Printed in Victoria, BC, Canada. Printed on paper with minimum 30% recycled fibre. Trafford's print shop runs on "green energy" from solar, wind and other environmentally-friendly power sources.

Offices in Canada, USA, Ireland and UK

This book was published *on-demand* in cooperation with Trafford Publishing. On-demand publishing is a unique process and service of making a book available for retail sale to the public taking advantage of on-demand manufacturing and Internet marketing. On-demand publishing includes promotions, retail sales, manufacturing, order fulfilment, accounting and collecting royalties on behalf of the author.

Book sales for North America and international:
Trafford Publishing, 6E–2333 Government St.,
Victoria, BC V8T 4P4 CANADA
phone 250 383 6864 (toll-free 1 888 232 4444)
fax 250 383 6804; email to orders@trafford.com

Book sales in Europe:
Trafford Publishing (UK) Limited, 9 Park End Street, 2nd Floor
Oxford, UK OX1 1HH UNITED KINGDOM
phone 44 (0)1865 722 113 (local rate 0845 230 9601)
facsimile 44 (0)1865 722 868; info.uk@trafford.com

Order online at:
trafford.com/05-1739

10 9 8 7 6 5 4 3 2

WHY YOU NEED AN ADVERTISEMENT RESUME!

Are you looking for a job and find yourself in one of these categories?

1. I'm losing my home because I can't make my mortgage payments after losing my job.
2. I'm a recent graduate and my resume doesn't seem to be getting any attention.
3. I'm going through a divorce because I can't support my family after losing my job.
4. I paid a lot of money to get a resume prepared, but got no responses.
5. I heard I had an **obituary resume**, how do I fix it?
6. I've never written a resume before, what do I need to say?

Are you in any of these situations?
You need to write an advertisement resume and **Make Your Resume Talk** for you.

First, you need to re-think who you are and learn to describe how good you are (**brag a little**). Then you need to build your resume section by section using the guidelines in this book. The book gives instructions, examples, and a place to draft your resume right after reading the guidelines. You will find that your revised resume will tell your story and what you can do for a potential employer. To get interviews and a job, you must tailor your resume specifically to each job you want to get.

I talked to officials at various types of businesses to see what made them read a resume and what made them throw a resume away. The feedback was clear and distinct: make the resumes short and describe your tasks and skills with results that jump out to entice the reviewer to read more than the initial 30-second review. This results in the advertisement resume that is written when you follow the guidelines in this book.

You have 30 seconds, if you're lucky, to get someone to want to read more about you. Your resume is simply an advertisement of who you are and the talents that you can bring to a potential employer. Writing an historical, obituary-type resume will get little attention and not excite a reader. You need to tell the reader how successful you have been in your previous work. Your bulleted work statements will give the potential employer a perspective of how well you can perform similar tasks and deliver results.

It is not easy to write statements about yourself, but that is what needs to be done to **Make Your Resume Talk** for you. Start now to write a resume that describes your experience, skills, and accomplishments. Make it an advertisement that you are proud of and tells a story of who you really are.

Many recruiters and Human Resources officers want your complete work history. You, no doubt, have already written a reverse-chronological resume so don't throw it away. Just be sure the longer reverse-chronological resume includes more than just your tasks. You can take it to an interview or use it for your work-history purposes. The advertisement resume is the easy-to-read, honest, targeted instrument you need to interest and entice potential employers to want to interview you.

YOU MUST ADVERTISE YOURSELF!
TODAY IT IS A STANDARD!

DO IT NOW!

I AM READY TO SHOW YOU HOW TO WRITE AN EFFECTIVE RESUME! YOUR ONLY REQUIREMENT IS TO ACCEPT THE CHALLENGE.

DO YOU REALLY WANT AN INTERVIEW AND A JOB?

Is your job search producing results? Don't send out the same stale copy of your resume, with a generalized cover letter, that you've used dozens of times with no results. This time, make the effort and **Make Your Resume Talk** to the HR Director or hiring manager about the position you want. You must sell your desire to get an interview for the position.

See the key points that advertise you and get you the interview.   **(Chapter 1)**
    The only purpose of your resume is to compel the reader to interview you.
    Rule of thumb: The first third of the resume must grab the reader's attention.
    The resume must be tailored to the specific needs of the employer.
    Every line should reinforce your ability to drive the reader to interview you.

What is an Obituary Resume?   **(Chapter 2)**
    An obituary resume is one that won't get read.
    It is full of task statements with no results.
    It does not entice a reader to interview you.

How can an employer reach you?   **(Chapter 3)**
    Include name, address, phone numbers, and e-mail address.
    Your name should be the biggest font in the heading.
    Your name should be the first thing on your resume.
    All information in the heading should be balanced.

You must target your Objective to the specific job and company.   **(Chapter 4)**
    List specific job and company.
    Include the experience and skills you bring to that job.
    Not more than 3 lines long.
    All of your Objective (headline) should be **boldface.**

Support your targeted Objective with your work statements.   **(Chapter 5)**
    Put job title, location, and dates on one line.
    Use action verbs and bulleted statements (no paragraphs).
    Show the task performed, skills used, and results obtained.

Do you have any computer skills?   **(Chapter 6)**
    Give an honest appraisal of your skill level.
    A technical addendum helps if you have extensive skills.

The Education section supports your experience and skills.   **(Chapter 7)**
    List formal education only.
    Include your degree, major, school, location, dates on one line.
    Leave off your graduation date if it is more than 10 years ago.

Activities give insight into your personal chemistry.   **(Chapter 8)**
    Use 3 or 4 maximum.
    Do not list religious or political items.

References are not part of your resume. (Chapter 11)
    References are needed, but they are not part of the resume.
    Get permission from the 3 references you need.
    Have your reference list at the interview on a separate sheet of paper.

High school students, without experience, need help too. (Chapter 12)
    Show mental ability plus energy and persistence in projects.
    Add computer skills, languages, and physical fitness.

College students must show what they have to offer, not what they want. (Chapter 13)
    GPA, if over 3.0, needs to be shown.
    Show internship or work experience. If none, show work on projects.
    Add leadership, computer skills, languages, and fitness items.

Flavor your resume if you're changing careers. (Chapter 14)
    Write to the new industry and transfer your skills.

Electronic resumes must be prepared differently. (Chapter 18)
    E-resumes are different from hard-copy resumes.
    Transform hard copy and test it before sending.

One student's personal feedback after using guidelines:

"I am sitting here looking at the old resume and the new resume prepared based on your guidelines".

"First, I can see a difference like you wouldn't believe".

"I showed it to my wife and she even said it looked great, and it was honest, too".

"I could go on and on, but just wanted to say 'Thanks' for the guidelines that transformed my dull and boring resume to an advertisement that is already getting me interviews."

Table of Contents

		Page Number
	Why You Need an Advertisement Resume!	i
	Do You Really Want an Interview and a Job?	iii
Chapter 1	Struggling with Your Resume?	1
Chapter 2	What Is an Obituary Resume?	3
Chapter 3	Heading – Who Are You?	7
Chapter 4	Target Your Objective	11
Chapter 5	Work Experience/Life Experience – Sell Yourself	15
Chapter 6	What Is Your Computer Skill Level?	27
Chapter 7	What to Include in the Education Section	31
Chapter 8	Activities Are Critical to Your Resume	35
Chapter 9	Were You in Military Service?	39
Chapter 10	Optional Items on a Resume	41
Chapter 11	References	43
Chapter 12	High School Students Need Help Too!	45
Chapter 13	College Graduates Are in the Middle	51
Chapter 14	Changing Careers? Flavor Your Resume	67
Chapter 15	Returning to a Job You Used to Do	77
Chapter 16	You Must Tailor Your Resume to a Specific Job	83
Chapter 17	Bonus: Short, Action Cover Letters	89
Chapter 18	Physical Attributes of a Resume	95
Chapter 19	How to Prepare an E-Resume	99
Chapter 20	Are You Really Employable?	105
Chapter 21	Frequently Asked Questions	107
	Hart's 25 Reminder's Checklist 109	109

	Page Number
Appendixes	
Appendix-A	110-150
Before and After Resume Examples with Critiques of the Before Versions	
Appendix-B	151-152
Background on Book and Layout	
Appendix-C	153
Testimonials	
Appendix-D	154-155
Why I Wrote this Book	
Appendix-E	156
Acknowledgements	
Appendix-F	157
About the Author	
Index	158
Reviewers' Comments	Back Cover

 Use "Hart's Tip's" and "Richard's Critiques" and "Richard's Reminders" to keep you on track as you write or re-write your resume.

CHAPTER
STRUGGLING WITH YOUR RESUME?

Did you struggle when you wrote a resume for the first time?

Did you mail 100 copies without any action?

Have you found it difficult to tailor your resume to a specific job?

Using this book will give you directions and confidence to write an effective advertising resume.

Look at the job Objectives in these two examples and see if they tell you what job the person wants, where he or she wants it, or what experience and skills the applicant has to offer a potential employer.

Example 1
"Seeking a challenging position where I can grow my company's revenue and have a chance for advancement."

Example 2
Software Design Engineer with the ABC Company bringing 15+ years of experience and skills in planning, designing, problem solving, and working with all company divisions that put a competitive product on the market. Fluent in Spanish and English.

Read each one again and see which one gets your attention. The first one is so general that an employer has no idea what the applicant wants or what he or she has to offer. The second one is a targeted Objective and lists the specific job the applicant is applying for, the company he or she wants to work for, and the experience and skills that the applicant has to offer that company. This Objective will get the attention of the reader.

The contents of this book

will train you to write

resumes that talk for you.

You are an important and unique individual.

Don't just try to copy a resume from this book.

STRUGGLING WITH YOUR RESUME?

(What you put in this space - the top 1/3 of your resume - is **critical**.)

 I use the **"Rule of Thumb"** line. That means if you pick up the resume in your hand so you can read it, you will probably pick it up with about 1/3 of the page above your thumb as shown.

If you have not captured the interest of a potential employer by the time you read down to your thumb, your resume will quickly go in the trash can. Therefore, it is imperative that you read the instructions for how to write an advertisement resume and use the tips given in this book to write a great resume. **You are not there to say, "What I meant to say was….". All you have in front of a potential employer is the piece of paper your resume is written on. It needs to talk for you and advertise the experience and skills you have and how good you were or are so that you will get the interview.**

I have read thousands of resumes that I classify as an **obituary resume**. They show an applicant's work history in reverse-chronological order and only show tasks and responsibilities. **Many people ask me why I use the word "obituary resume" because it seems so final. I use that term because I want you to realize it is final if your resume is presented incorrectly and does nothing for you.** I genuinely want you to take a fresh look at who you are and this book will give you the opportunity to find yourself, your talent, and how you can write your findings to show who you and your talents really are. Following the guidelines in this book will transform your resume and, I believe, your career. (See Chapter 2 on what is meant by the term "obituary resume.") Most people grab a book or pay someone to write their resumes without thinking what they really have on their resumes.

There are certain sections of the resume that I think are essential–the Heading, Objective, Work Experience, Computer Skills (if applicable), Education, Military Service (if applicable), and Activities. Each one is explained in a different chapter with guidelines and examples to show what is meant and how to visualize and write an advertisement resume. Optional items (summary, memberships, awards or honors, and licenses) are addressed in Chapter 10.

TAKE ACTION

I'm asking you to read your own resume critically and see if it is interesting and enticing enough to keep reading.

If not, you have missed the real purpose of the resume and that is to get you an interview.

You must reconsider what you have written and what needs to be changed. Then, using the guidelines in this book, write or re-write the necessary material to Make Your Resume Talk for you.

CHAPTER 2
WHAT IS AN OBITUARY RESUME?

We mentioned an obituary resume in the last chapter. The differences between an obituary resume and an advertisement resume are explained in this chapter.

Objective statements
When you think of the Objective, you are programmed to write down the job you want. That is not enough today. Here are some examples of obituary Objectives:

"Entry-level accountant"

This is considered an obituary Objective because it states only what position the applicant is trying to get. What skills does the applicant have to offer? Does this Objective get you excited or interested to read any more of the resume?

"To coach and teach at the high school level"

This one is a little more explanatory but is still an obituary Objective. It states what the person wants but says nothing about what they are qualified to do or what they have to offer. Has the applicant ever coached before or have they ever taught before? If so, what sports did they coach or what subjects did they teach? Is a reviewer going to find out the answers to these questions in 30 seconds?

"Senior Marketing/Sales Manager position utilizing an extensive, successful foundation with global leaders in consumer electronics, providing energetic, performance-driven creative team leadership."

This one really sounds good, but it is still an obituary Objective. When you read it closely, it is all historical and says nothing about what skills the applicant has to offer a potential employer. This one might get a little more attention but will it capture the interest of a reviewer to get an interview? Also, the term Sales Manager is a "position" so this applicant has duplicated words that will not help.

WHAT IS AN OBITUARY RESUME?

Work Experience statements

These Work Experience statements further explain what is meant by an obituary resume.

BEFORE
"Responsible for selling a portfolio of bank services B2B."

This statement only says what the person is supposed to do, and there is no indication that the applicant actually did what they were responsible for. How good was the person in doing this task? Nothing is shown to indicate any results from the task. Compare the "before" to the "after."

AFTER
"Sold a portfolio of bank services B2B that increased sales by 16% in first year."

BEFORE
"Called on by other company divisions to lead and train their HR teams."

"To" is like "responsible for." It again states what the person is supposed to do, not what they actually did. No achievement or result is shown for this task or if the person performed successfully.

AFTER
"Called on by other company divisions to lead and train their HR teams that resulted in increased and uniform knowledge about the new methods of customer service dictated by management."

BEFORE
"Installed updated software programs and maintained daily logs."

This covers two tasks but has nothing to say about how well the tasks were performed or what happened as a result of doing the task. It would help if the applicant could show how quickly the software was installed. Was it done successfully and did anyone use the logs to make changes or decisions for future work?

AFTER
"Installed updated software on division's 120 computers in 2 days and maintained daily logs that were combined and personally analyzed, with resulting reports sent to the Division Chief for immediate or future action."

These are simple examples, but they say a lot about why obituary Objectives and obituary Work Experience statements do not talk for you and do not advertise your skills to get anyone excited enough to contact you for an interview.

Does the obituary resume on the next page resemble your resume? If so, the contents of this book are just the thing for you to learn how to write a resume to get a reviewer excited about what you have to offer a potential employer. You must use CPR and pump some life into your resume and bring it to life. This is what gets you interviews and a job.

Example of an Obituary Resume

Richard A. Marks
1234 Jones Street, Raleigh, NC 27513   (919) 989-4321   rmarks@home.net

Objective
An industrial engineering position with sufficient breadth of accountability to achieve a significant increase in business profits. Ideally, success would require fast and accurate assessment of customer/prospect situations, strong interpersonal skills to build long-term relationships, and the ability to sell effectively at all levels.

Career Summary
A results driven Sales engineer combining strong communication, innovation, and technology capabilities to achieve customer satisfaction and sales targets. Ability to lead and manage complex projects using a team-oriented approach. Proven track record of winning new customers to grow sales and profits.

Work Experience

Alright Specialty Sales, Charlotte, NC   1996-2005
<u>Outside Sales</u> – Called on over 500 customers in the Carolinas to sell tool steels, other specialty metals, and related services. Customers included large OEMs, tool & die shops and custom equipment fabricators. Buying contacts were business owners, project managers, and tool & die makers.

Hixson Corporation, Morristown, NJ   1985-1996
<u>Manager, Sales Marketing and Government Affairs</u> – Introduced and sold quenched steel strip to electrical equipment manufacturers as a replacement for grain oriented electrical steel.
- Developed and implemented sales and marketing strategy including pricing, promotion, target markets, key customers and end user influence.
- Recruited, trained, and managed the sales team of regional sales managers, financial and engineering analysts, and technical service specialists.
- Negotiated sales contracts, development agreements, and technology licenses.
- Promoted product sales with presentations to customers, industry groups, and government officials.

United Technologies, East Hartford, CT   1981-1985
<u>Senior Metallurgist</u> – Managed Navy and Air Force funded programs to develop production processes for directionally solidified in-site composite turbine blades.
- Implemented processes to increase the production speed and yield of critical jet engine parts and developed technology to manufacture columnar grain and single turbine blades.

Education
Rensselaer Polytechnic Institute, MS – Metallurgy
Rutgers University, BS – Ceramic Science

Author's Note – If you read all the information on this resume, you will see that there is not one achievement or anything else that says how good this applicant is.

The "to" statements are what the person was responsible for, not what they actually did. This is a Basic Obituary Resume.

WHAT IS AN OBITUARY RESUME?

* Notes *

CHAPTER 3
HEADING – WHO ARE YOU?

The Heading starts your resume and is important because it contains the information for a potential employer to get in touch with you. The format used will depend on what you have to say on your resume and how much space you have.

Normally you have six lines of information in your heading, as follows:

Name	Richard A. Hart
Address – (2 lines)	600 New Waverly Place
	Cary, NC 27511
Home phone	(919) 851-xxxx
Cell phone	(919) 304-xxxx
E-mail address	rahart@aol.com

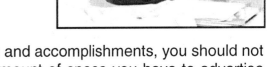

If you have lots of experience, many jobs, or many results and accomplishments, you should not use 6 lines for your heading because that will limit the amount of space you have to advertise your experience and accomplishments.

You can use as large as 14-pt font for your name and you should make your name bold, using all caps. The font size for the rest of the heading can be as small as 8-pt font but use common sense in the size selected. Make it easy to read, but also remember that your name is the most important part in the first reading. (See Chapter 18 for the physical attributes of a resume.)

If you do not use the 6-line format above, you need to be sure you balance whatever format you use. Here are some examples:

RICHARD A. HART
600 New Waverly Place, Cary, NC 27511   (919) 851-xxxx(h)   (919) 304-xxxx(c)   rahart@aol.com

---

RICHARD A. HART

| 600 New Waverly Place | | (day) (919) 304-xxxx |
| Cary, NC 27511 | rahart@aol.com | (evening) (919) 851-xxxx |

Note: Balanced horizontally (evenly weighted) but used day and evening for phone numbers so potential employer may have to make only one phone call.

RICHARD A. HART

| (919) 851-xxxx | 600 New Waverly Place | rahart@aol.com |
| | Cary, NC 27511 | |

Note: This format can be used when an applicant has only a home phone or cell phone and an e-mail address.

Use your own judgment when selecting the format.

HEADING – WHO ARE YOU?

You will note that in all the examples the name is the top item and the first thing one reads in the heading. This is not happenstance. If a resume is computer-scanned and your name is not distinctively above the rest of your information in the heading, you will appear as "600 New Waverly Place" or (919) 851-xxxx if your resume is selected by the computer for further review. That is why **your name must be first and above everything else on your resume.**

 Ugly resumes won't get read and the first indication of this is in your Heading and whether or not you balance the information shown.

 Please do not use lines or double lines clear across the page in your heading or under your heading or any place else on the resume because such lines may stop a computer scan of your resume.

 Cute or humorous e-mail addresses are not professional and could mean that you are not serious about getting a job. In the examples throughout this book, you will see that the e-mail addresses are all business-like.

 The same holds true for your phone-answering machine. If you are not working, the following message is suggested for your answering machine. "I am not home right now as I am out looking for a job as a software developer [or whatever job you are looking for]. If you have any leads to help me, please leave me a message with your phone number so I can call you back as soon as I return. If you have no leads, leave me a friendly message and I'll call you back."

Once, you have finished the heading, one of the easiest parts of the resume is finished. Now, let's talk about the next and hardest part to write – the OBJECTIVE. The Objective clearly differentiates an advertisement resume from the obituary resume.

TAKE ACTION

Using the guidelines above, use the format on the next page to visualize and <u>write your heading</u>.

We will use this format throughout the book to get you to write each section right after you read the instruction.

HEADING – WHO ARE YOU?

HEADING

OBJECTIVE

WORK EXPERIENCE

COMPUTER SKILLS

EDUCATION

ACTIVITIES

HART'S REMINDERS

☐ Did you bold your name and use all caps?

☐ Did you use 6 lines when 2 lines would allow more space for information related to landing an interview?

☐ Is your Heading format pleasing to the eye?

HEADING – WHO ARE YOU?
* NOTES *

CHAPTER 4
TARGET YOUR OBJECTIVE

When you write an Objective, write a targeted Objective. A targeted Objective has three parts:

1. Targeted job
2. Targeted company
3. Experience and skills you can bring to the targeted job

Targeted job
If you are applying for a specific job, use the job title or wording shown in the job or vacancy announcement. This is especially true if the resumes are going to be computer scanned for key words. It is also imperative that you use the company's job title to be sure you are being considered for the right job in case the company is trying to fill more than one vacancy.

Targeted company
If you are sending the resume to a specific company, put that company's name in the Objective to show you want to work for them. If you do not know the company's name or are going to attend a job fair and do not know which companies will be represented, leave the name out of the Objective on some of the resumes. It is very difficult to get any response from a general "fishing" resume. A "fishing" resume is a resume where an applicant describes in detail the type of job and job features he or she is looking for in hopes that the reader will "catch on" to what the applicant wants. In a competitive market, this type of resume will not get you the desired interview.

If you do not know the company's name, use a reverse phone listing or e-mail lookup on the Internet and this might get you the company's name. That shows some extra effort on your part and will put your resume in a different pile immediately. And, please spell the name of the company correctly.

Experience and skills you can bring to a targeted job
Show the number of years experience and the skills you can offer to do the targeted job. If you have more than 15 years experience, show 15+ years in your Objective to try to get away from age discrimination. Use the plus sign (+) rather than saying "more than" or "plus" as it is more eye-catching and will be remembered by the reviewer. Experience is still "what have you done lately?" so the emphasis in the targeted objective and the resume as a whole is the most recent 12-15 years.

One of the biggest problems with most Objectives is that they do not say what the applicant has to offer a potential employer. Most Objectives are too general and describe the type of job the applicant wants or the type of job he or she has done in the past and don't get the attention of a Human Resources person or hiring manager.

TARGET YOUR OBJECTIVE

Many HR representatives read only the Objective on a resume. If it is good and enticing, the reviewer will read on. If the Objective is too general and doesn't say what you have to offer as experience and skills, the resume will quickly go in the trash can.

Something that might help you understand the Objective better is to consider it as a headline in a newspaper. You know that when you read a newspaper you glance at the headlines on a page and skip ones that aren't interesting or ones that don't entice you to read on. This scenario is just like the resume process.

An Objective that doesn't say anything, or is not enticing or interesting to a potential employer, doesn't get read (the 15-30 second reading) and there are no appeals to get it back out of the trash can. Therefore, it is critical that you include the experience and skills you have to offer a potential employer in your Objective.

The Objective is the hardest part of the resume to write and must be written first. Too many people write their Work Experience section first in a task-oriented fashion and then try to go back and write an Objective to fit both their experience and those jobs they are applying for. This is most difficult and usually doesn't work because the Objective doesn't agree with the work statements they have drafted.

You must write the Objective first and tailor it to the job you are applying for. Then write your Work Experience to show you have performed the needed skills stated in your tailored, targeted Objective.

You are probably wondering, "How long should the Objective or headline be?" It should not be more than 3 lines long (not 3 sentences). Yes, it will be a fragmented statement, but most headlines are just that. Your complete Objective (or headline) should be made **bold** so it jumps out at the reader. The only time you should have more than one statement is if you have a language or special qualification to add (i.e., "Fluent in Spanish and English," or "Sign language," or "Notary Public.") These would make you more valuable and different from the other applicants and should help you get an interview.

Compare the following Objectives to see why it is important to show the targeted job, targeted company, and the experience and skills you have to offer a potential employer. The last Objective is the preferred one, but you need to read through all of them to compare what you have written and then see what is needed to target your resume to a specific job.

(a) Senior Accountant

This is only a job title and is too general and doesn't tell what experience, if any, the applicant has. It is not going to get a reader to go any further and does not include the skills the applicant has to offer.

TARGET YOUR OBJECTIVE

(b) Senior Accountant with experience in tax, corporate, foundation, and international accounting.

The Objective does list the position applied for but is historical and lists areas of experience from the past. It does not show the skills that the applicant has to offer.

(c) Seeking a senior accounting position where I can use my experience in tax, corporate, foundation, and international accounting to grow the company's revenue and advance into a management position.

This Objective lists the job the person wants rather than the experience and skills the applicant has to offer. Also, it is written in first person rather than third person. You do not need to say "seeking," as the resume is a seeking document itself. Start with the job title that is shown in the vacancy or job announcement. This will help if a computer scan is used and also help if the company has more than one job available that you might be qualified for. In the latter case, you will have to submit a different resume for each job and tailor the resume to the specifics of each job.

(d) Senior Accountant with the ABC Company bringing 15+ years of experience and skills in tax, corporate, foundation, and international accounting plus correcting errors that get unqualified opinions.

This is a targeted Objective that shows the targeted job, targeted company, and the experience and skills the applicant has to offer a potential employer. Each Objective will be different for each applicant, as people are different and have different experience and skills to offer. Some may not have recent education, some may not have certifications (such as CPA), and some may be fluent in a foreign language or sign language. These skills that apply to your targeted job make you different and better qualified and need to be worked into your Objective.

A targeted Objective sets the structure for the rest of your resume as you must support your different experiences and skills (and include how good you were or are) in your Work Experience section. Using Objective (d) above, you would need to show you have 15+ years of experience and describe your skills in tax, corporate, foundation, and international accounting and what you did and how good you were. This must also include the type of errors you found and how you got them corrected to get the unqualified opinions on a company's financial statements.

TAKE ACTION

Now you need to visualize your Objective

and write one on the next page that is

targeted, enticing, and definitely shows

what you have to offer a potential employer.

TARGET YOUR OBJECTIVE

HEADING

OBJECTIVE

WORK EXPERIENCE

COMPUTER SKILLS

EDUCATION

ACTIVITIES

HART'S REMINDERS

- ☐ Did you write a targeted Objective with a targeted job, targeted company, and the experience and skills you can bring to the targeted job?
- ☐ Is your Objective an offering one rather than an historical or seeking Objective?
- ☐ Is your Objective (Headline) 3 lines or less?

CHAPTER 5
WORK / LIFE EXPERIENCE – SELL YOURSELF

As you build or re-write your resume, the Work Experience section must support your targeted Objective and show that you have the skills and are good enough to deserve an interview. **Remember, your resume only gets you the interview, not the job.** Therefore, how you write your Work Experience to support the skills stated in your targeted Objective is critical.

Let's start with your job title and where you worked and when. It all goes on one line.

Job title (bold), name of company, location, and dates worked. For example,
Senior Accountant, ABC Company, Raleigh, NC   1992-2004

Job titles are self-descriptive and give a potential employer an idea of what you have done before reading anything else about you. Making the job title **bold** also helps make it jump out at the reader.

Many official job titles are not very descriptive of what you really did and may hurt you because the reader doesn't really know what you actually did. Titles such as Assistant Director, Group Director, Manager, or Area Supervisor all sound important but are very bland in relation to what you did. There is nothing wrong with adding a word to make the titles say something about you. Revising the earlier titles to Assistant Director for Auditing, Group Planning Director, Sales Manager, and Manufacturing Area Supervisor are much more descriptive of what you really did and mean much more to a potential employer.

You may have had more than one job title with a company but list only the latest title unless you have had critical titles/jobs with one company that supports your current targeted Objective. You are trying to show you have experience that supports your current Objective without showing all the titles with the previous company that might duplicate what you did. Occasionally you might need to use two titles, such as Software Developer/Test Engineer, to show what you have done that supports what you want to do next.

You would show it this way:
Software Developer/Test Engineer, ABC Company, Raleigh, NC   15+ years

Use the name of the company that you worked for. If the company was sold after you worked for them, use the name of the new company, as your records are probably still on file there. Do not show both company names. It is also not necessary to say the company went out of business or with whom it merged. It just makes the reviewer read more words that don't advertise you or how good you are. You do not need to use the street address or zip code for the company, only the town and state.

 Hart's Tip: Put your dates to the far right. It is more important to show the job title that supports your targeted job first. The time information is needed, but is less important than the other information.

WORK / LIFE EXPERIENCE – SELL YOURSELF

There are different ways to show your dates, but remember that "what you have done lately" is most important. Any work experience past 12-15 years is not as relevant as your recent experience. In that case, you want to show no more than 15+ years of experience in detail with tasks and results. You can either use calendar dates or years to support your time working. Rewriting the previous Senior Accountant job could be shown as:

Senior Accountant, ABC Company, Raleigh, NC   12 years

There are times that older experience best supports what you want to do now. Using the years rather than the calendar dates would help in those instances. In such cases, you would not put your Work Experience in reverse-chronological order, but move up your best experience so it will support your targeted Objective sooner and show the number of years and not the calendar dates. However, when you fill out the company's application, you will have to go back to the reverse-chronological order and use calendar dates. The resume has already served its purpose and got you the interview and the chance to fill out an application.

Your experience is the key to getting your next job, but it is difficult for older applicants to compete with younger applicants. Therefore, check all dates or years shown on your resume to be consistent and to be sure you are no more than 37+ years old on your resume. For example, don't take the dates off your education to hide your age and then say you started to work in 1970 or you were in the Military Service from 1968-1972.

Students could graduate from college at age 22 so adding 15+ years of work experience would only show you are 37+ years old. Older applicants should also show only 15+ years of experience in order to not be unfairly screened out of consideration.

If you use calendar dates on your resume, you may have some unexplained gaps in your Work Experience. Sometimes using years/years rather than months / years will eliminate small time gaps.

See the following examples to show the months/years format versus the years/years format:

<u>Months/years format</u>
Electronic Engineer, ABC Company, Chicago, IL   7/1997-9/2004
Entry-level Engineer, XYZ Company, Milwaukee, WI   1/1995-1/1997

This shows a gap in employment of 6 months and will have to be explained.

<u>Revised to years/years format</u>
Electronic Engineer, ABC Company, Chicago, IL   1997-2004
Entry-level Engineer, XYZ Company, Milwaukee, WI   1995-1997

The years to years format may also mask longer time gaps. Using the above example but changing the years would give you these results.

<u>Months/years format</u>
Electronic Engineer, ABC Company, Chicago, IL   7/1997-9/2004
Entry-level Engineer, XYZ Company, Milwaukee, WI   1/1995-1/1996

WORK / LIFE EXPERIENCE – SELL YOURSELF

This shows a gap of 18 months.

Revised to years/years format
Electronic Engineer, ABC Company, Chicago, IL   1997-2004
Entry-level Engineer, XYZ Company, Milwaukee, WI   1995-1996

Although there is an 18-month difference shown in the first example, one cannot readily tell that there is a gap in the second example. The second format (years to years) does not show a time gap in employment. However, if you fill out an application when you go in for an interview, you will be asked to show months, days, and years for all previous jobs and the gaps will appear. But your resume has done its job; it got you the interview, and you will have to re-sell your experience and skills and show what you can do for that employer during the interview.

Recent graduates or younger applicants can use calendar dates (not just years) without having to worry about the age factor.

How to write your Work Experience statements
Read the vacancy announcements closely to see what the experience requirements are for each job you want to apply for and honestly tailor your work statements to fit those requirements.

This section must be carefully written and it needs to show the benefits or results for the tasks you have performed. Do not write your Work Experience in paragraphs as the most important thing in your paragraph is probably the last line and most reviewers will not read that far. Please write your experience using individual bulleted statements. Each statement must be self-contained and not refer to statements above or below.

Use past-tense action verbs for tasks completed and present-tense action verbs on current tasks to lead in to each bulleted statement and show the task performed, skill used, and results YOU achieved for each task. You do not have to show every task you worked on, so be selective and use the tasks and results that best advertise your skills to a potential employer. You may have to combine some tasks to get a result.

A potential employer wants to know how good your skills are and what value you can bring to his/her business. Stating results or accomplishments is the best way to show this mandatory item. Most resume writers have never thought about their accomplishments because it wasn't necessary when jobs were plentiful or available. In addition, you probably remember hearing your mother say, "Butch (Susie), never brag on yourself; let your work speak for you."

 Bragging about yourself is OK now. You definitely need to advertise your skills and successes to get an interview for your next job.

One student sent the following message back to me. "This week, I had 2 interviews. Rewriting my resume incorporating the concise, forward-promoting (not historically-documenting) methods of writing my Work Experience with results that Dick Hart teaches surely made the difference in attracting these employment opportunities."

WORK / LIFE EXPERIENCE – SELL YOURSELF

The results or achievements should specify quality, quantity, production, or cost/revenue facts.

> **Quality** (how accurate, how quick, how good)
> **Quantity** (how many, how much above normal or quota)
> **Production** (number produced in a certain time period)
> **Cost/Revenue** (changes made that decreased cost or effort expended that increased revenue and by how much)

 Sometimes percentages are better indicators of increases than dollar amounts. If dollar amounts are used, please use the dollar sign ($) and numbers as they are more eye-catching and memorable than writing out the amounts.

WORK / LIFE EXPERIENCE – SELL YOURSELF

Interview yourself to help write your resume

 Hart's Tip: Most people cannot write about themselves and staring at your resume or scratching your head won't put the proper words on your resume.

My suggestion is to get a **voice recorder** or **VCR** and have a friend interview you using the following questions.

Write down the results after listening to the feedback.

Talking through and about your work will bring back things that have been forgotten but are needed now to advertise you.

Then you can tie your successes to the tasks on your draft resume and **Make Your Resume Talk** for you.

If management by objectives was used on prior jobs, you should review your past performance reviews to see if they include your accomplishments.

Here are Richard's Top 10 Questions to ask yourself when trying to get a result for each task written on your current resume.

1. How good was I?
2. What happened as a result of performing the project or task?
3. Did I save any money or increase revenue as a result of my effort?
4. How accurate was I?
5. Was I ahead of schedule or did I just meet the schedule?
6. Did I supervise people? How many? Did I train or motivate them?
7. Did I exceed my quota? Show me the numbers.
8. What was my role on the team?
9. What impact did I make?
10. Do Results jump out at the reviewer? and Would I hire me?

WORK / LIFE EXPERIENCE – SELL YOURSELF

ACTION VERBS

The following lists of action verbs are provided to help you in writing your Work Experience statements. Do not overuse a particular word. Read through the complete list. Seeing the words may jog your memory about something good that you did but had forgotten in your haste to get the resume written. The lists are categorized to make it easier to find the word that best fits what you did.

Financial Skills

administered	adjusted	allocated	analyzed	appraised	assessed	audited
balanced	budgeted	calculated	computed	conserved	corrected	determined
developed	estimated	forecasted	managed	marketed	measured	planned
prepared	programmed	projected	reconciled	reduced	researched	retrieved

Management/Leadership Skills

achieved	administered	analyzed	appointed	approved	assigned	attained
authorized	chaired	consolidated	contracted	controlled	converted	coordinated
delegated	developed	directed	eliminated	emphasized	enforced	enhanced
established	executed	expanded	generated	headed	hired	hosted
improved	incorporated	increased	initiated	inspected	instituted	led
managed	motivated	organized	originated	overhauled	oversaw	planned
presided	prioritized	produced	reduced	reorganized	replaced	restored
reviewed	scheduled	secured	selected	spearheaded	streamlined	
strengthened	supervised	surpassed	terminated	transferred	recommended	

Organization/Detail Skills

approved	arranged	catalogued	categorized	charted	classified	coded
collected	compiled	corrected	distributed	executed	filed	corresponded
generated	implemented	incorporated	inspected	logged	maintained	monitored
obtained	operated	ordered	organized	prepared	processed	provided
purchased	recorded	registered	reserved	responded	reviewed	routed
scheduled	screened	setup	submitted	standardized	systematized	updated
validated	verified	won				

Research Skills

analyzed	clarified	collected	compared	completed	conducted	critiqued
detected	determined	diagnosed	evaluated	examined	explored	experimented
extracted	formulated	gathered	identified	inspected	interpreted	interviewed
invented	investigated	located	measured	organized	researched	reviewed
searched	solved	summarized	surveyed	systematized	tested	

Communication/People Skills

addressed	advertised	arbitrated	arranged	authored	clarified	collaborated
composed	condensed	conferred	consulted	contacted	conveyed	corresponded
convinced	debated	defined	described	developed	directed	discussed
drafted	edited	elicited	enlisted	explained	expressed	formulated
incorporated	influenced	interacted	interpreted	interviewed	involved	joined
judged	lectured	listened	marketed	mediated	moderated	negotiated
observed	outlined	persuaded	presented	promoted	proposed	publicized
reconciled	recruited	referred	reinforced	reported	resolved	responded
solicited	specified	spoke	suggested	summarized	synthesized	translated
wrote						

WORK / LIFE EXPERIENCE – SELL YOURSELF

Helping Skills

adapted	advocated	answered	arranged	assessed	cared for	clarified
coached	contributed	counseled	diagnosed	educated	ensured	demonstrated
encouraged	expedited	facilitated	guided	insured	intervened	motivated
referred	rehabilitated	resolved	simplified	supplied	supported	volunteered

Technical Skills

adapted	applied	assembled	built	calculated	computed	conserved
constructed	converted	debugged	designed	determined	developed	engineered
expanded	fabricated	fortified	installed	maintained	operated	overhauled
printed	programmed	rectified	regulated	remodeled	repaired	replaced
restored	solved	specialized	standardized	studied	tested	upgraded
utilized						

Teaching Skills

adapted	advised	clarified	coached	communicated	conducted
coordinated	critiqued	developed	enabled	encouraged	evaluated
exceeded	explained	facilitated	focused	guided	improved
individualized	informed	instilled	instructed	motivated	persuaded
reduced	set	simulated	stimulated	succeeded	taught
tested	trained	transmitted	tutored		

This area is for you to jot down ideas or other words

WORK / LIFE EXPERIENCE – SELL YOURSELF

 Hart's Tip: Many students have told me that the action verbs really made them think of tasks and results that they had forgotten.

The following are examples of Work Experience statements with results to show the kind of statements you need to write on your advertisement resume. Many other examples are shown on the "after" versions of resumes in the appendix.

- Initiated new direct sales policy for ABC Company that resulted in personal contact with clients and increased sales by $1 million the first full year of using the technique.

- Supervised 8 network engineers in development of research for digital technical systems that resulted in 5 patents for processes developed and all projects completed ahead of schedule.

- Served as service advisor for Northern Auto dealership and received only one complaint from customers in the last year.

- Exceeded sales quota by 15% for past year by gaining new customers and maintaining current customers while providing great customer service.

See how the action verbs set the scene for what you actually did.

 Hart's Tip: Sometimes you need to put the result first to vary your information and make the result more important than the task.

Many times individuals copy information from their job descriptions, which really hurts them on their resumes. The following tip will put this in perspective.

 Hart's Tip: Words like "Responsible for," "responsibilities included," and "duties included" are statements of what you were supposed to do and don't really indicate what you actually did.

You may have been responsible for many tasks, but really didn't do anything as you delegated the actual work to someone else. Therefore, only use things that **you** actually did and how well you performed those tasks. Please avoid statements that show responsibility and stick with actual work you performed.

Many times you use the word "to" leading into what your tasks accomplished. "To" used in this sense is just like "responsible for." If you actually did what you were supposed to do, use "that" and a past tense verb to show you actually accomplished the task and then add the result.

 Hart's Tip: PLEASE BE HONEST IN WHAT YOU SAY YOU DID AND YOUR ACCOMPLISHMENTS. DO NOT STRETCH OR FUDGE EITHER AREA. GETTING FIRED FOR LYING IS NOT WORTH THE RISK OF FUDGING OR STRETCHING WHAT YOU HONESTLY DID!

WORK / LIFE EXPERIENCE – SELL YOURSELF

Key Words or Buzz Words
"Key words" or "buzz words" are used by many resume writers to show that the applicant has experience and skills in special areas. However, most people who use "buzz words" just make a list of them somewhere on their resume. Unfortunately, there is no indication of the level of ability in each of the "buzz words" listed so the words sit on your resume as part of your obituary. You must bring these words to life to really provide any positive help in using them.

 Computer scanning has driven resume writers to use "key words" or buzz words" in the hope that listing the proper words will get their resumes to the top. Just listing them will not help you. You must use these words in what you did and what you accomplished.

One student told me he had gotten 52 hits on his computer-design position resume because he had listed all the "buzz words" he could in hopes of getting an interview. He then told me that he had received no calls for an interview even with the 52 hits. After listening to my discussion on using an advertisement resume, he then knew why he had not received any calls. The "buzz words" were meaningless without connecting them to results.

If "buzz words" are used on a resume, put them in your bulleted work statements and describe what you actually did in each area related to your "buzz words" and the achievements you had. Without writing your experience this way, you will not get anyone to read your resume even with the list of "buzz words."

The student mentioned above later sent the following e-mail message: **"After changing my resume to an advertisement and working the 'buzz words' into my work statements and adding results, I started to get many calls for interviews."**

When you write your Work Experience statements with tasks and achievements, you have already set yourself up well for your interviews because you can now talk about your successes much more easily.

 Including results in your resume is not an exercise; it is a necessity if you expect to get any action from your resume.

How to cover old experience
You do not have to list all the jobs you have had that are more than 15 years old. Even if you have been with the same company for longer than 15 years, you do not want to show you worked for 29 years or worked from 1976-2005. You would write it this way on the Job Title line:

Software Development Engineer, IBM, RTP, NC   1990-2005 (or 15+years)

Then you would write a statement like this:
Also worked as an engineer for IBM in NY

Or

Also worked as an engineer at IBM in NC, where problem-solving process was initiated.

Or it could involve many companies, written like this:

Also worked as a development engineer for various computer and engineering companies in NY, CA, and NC.

WORK / LIFE EXPERIENCE – SELL YOURSELF

Because the experience is old and may not be up-to-date technically, it helps if you say where else you have worked and provide a hint of what you did and how good you were. It may even be a longer statement, but it doesn't take a whole page of bulleted statements to write something that won't get read or won't help you get an interview. The write-up for old experience should not be more than two or three lines. See examples C, E, F, H, I, and J in the Appendix that show how to show old experience.

Stay-at-home Mom
If you have been a stay-at-home Mom and want to return to the workforce, you may be afraid this will hurt you on a resume. Be creative and do not show this time as a period of unemployment. You have developed many skills during this time that you can offer to a potential employer. Just because you were not paid doesn't mean you didn't work or learn anything.

I suggest you show this time period in the following manner.

Stay-at-home Mom, (location)   1998-2005 or 7 years
- Learned life skills in listening, time management, budgeting, negotiation, and problem solving that are present at every job performed.

You can list at least **five** skills you learned and show ones that help meet the advertised needs for the job you are targeting. Other possible skills are organization, financial management, event planning, instructing, mentoring, and coaching. (See examples on pages **81 and 116** .)

Volunteer experience
Many times your only working experience is in a volunteer capacity. This experience could be critical to getting a paid job now. You need to write what skills you developed and used as if you were in a paid position and follow the guidelines shown in Chapters 4 to 6 related to Objectives, Work Experience, and Computer Skills. The most important part is to describe what you did, how well you performed, and the impact you made to show the reader you have skills **and** deserve an interview.

TAKE ACTION

You need to visualize what tasks you have performed that fit the requirements for the specific job you are applying for and use the action verbs to lead in to your statements.

Also, you must think or re-think what happened as a result of the tasks you performed.

Now you are ready to write your Work Experience section on the following page.

WORK / LIFE EXPERIENCE – SELL YOURSELF

HEADING
OBJECTIVE

WORK EXPERIENCE

COMPUTER SKILLS
EDUCATION
ACTIVITIES

Make Your Resume Talk

HART'S REMINDERS

- ☐ Do your Work Experience statements indicate how good you were, quantify measurements of successes, and describe your impact within the organization?
- ☐ If you worked more than 15 years, have you disguised the time factor?
- ☐ Were you honest?
- ☐ Did you evaluate the skills needed for the targeted job and tailor your resume to support these skills?
- ☐ Did you combine job titles for the same company and not repeat duties?
- ☐ Did you just include the last 12-15 years of your work experience?

CHAPTER 6
WHAT IS YOUR COMPUTER SKILL LEVEL?

Most jobs now require knowledge of computers. How you show this information depends on the level of your ability and the different software, hardware, and application systems that you have used.

Computer skills are another way to differentiate you from your competitors. Just listing the information is not enough. You should show your skill level in each system, hardware, or software area that you have experience in. Also show your honest keyboarding speed if you are applying for an office or administrative position and your speed is more than 60 words per minute. The following is the minimum way to show your skill level if you do not have many areas to include.

COMPUTER SKILLS
Advanced in WORD, Excel, and the Internet
Intermediate in PowerPoint, Quicken, and Lotus 1-2-3
Knowledgeable in Visio and PageMaker
Keyboarding (65 wpm)

Providing this information shows your honest evaluation of how good you are in each of the areas. It is another example of advertising your skill level to the reader. Even if the job announcement does not say anything about computer skills, I suggest you add what you have as most jobs now are affected by the use of computers, and this might be a differentiator for you.

 For advanced computer users, the best way to show your computer ability is to use a Technical Addendum.

The following page shows an example of a completed Technical Addendum. There may be other ways to show your computer knowledge level, but you definitely need something to show your ability in comparison to your competitors.

WHAT IS YOUR COMPUTER SKILL LEVEL?

Name
Technical Addendum

Category	Experience Level	Last Used
Programming Languages		
Java	Skilled	Recently
Delphi (3 and 4)	Expert	Recently
MVS COBOL & JCL	Knowledgeable	Not recently
Visual Basic	Knowledgeable	Not recently
Database Systems		
NCR Teradata RDMS	Intermediate	Recently
Oracle	Intermediate	Recently
Access 2000	Intermediate	Recently
Web Technologies		
XML	Knowledgeable	Recently
JSP	Knowledgeable	Recently
MySQL	Knowledgeable	Recently
PHP 4.0	Knowledgeable	Recently
Selected Applications		
Dreamweaver/Ultradev 4	Knowledgeable	Recently
Forte for JAVA v3.0	Intermediate	Recently
MS Office applications	Intermediate	Recently
MS Project	Intermediate	Recently
Adobe Acrobat 5.0	Expert	Recently
MS FrontPage 2000	Intermediate	Not recently
Operating Systems		
Windows NT/2000	Intermediate	Recently
Unix	Knowledgeable	Not recently
MVS/VM	Knowledgeable	Not recently

 Hart's Tip If you have a lot of "Not recently" items (more than 2 years) listed in the third column, you might want to delete column 3 and show only your experience level with each category item listed.

Now, decide how you want to show your computer skills and either list them on the front of the resume or make them a Technical Addendum on page 2. The number of items listed may be the deciding factor. Be honest in the level of experience that you have. For resume writers who do not have enough technical experience to justify using a Technical Addendum, a format for Computer Skills is provided on the next page.

WHAT IS YOUR COMPUTER SKILL LEVEL?

HEADING

OBJECTIVE

WORK EXPERIENCE

COMPUTER SKILLS

Advanced in

Intermediate in

Knowledgeable in

EDUCATION

ACTIVITIES

HART'S REMINDERS

☐ Did you show your level of ability for your computer skills?

☐ Were you honest in showing your level of ability for computer skills?

WHAT IS YOUR COMPUTER SKILL LEVEL?
* NOTES *

CHAPTER 7
WHAT TO INCLUDE IN THE EDUCATION SECTION

This is the easiest section to write, but you need to be selective in what you want to show. List only formal education in this section. (Training may appear in another place.) If you attended a school of learning past high school, but didn't graduate, list it. That could be another differentiator in comparison with another applicant.

 Hart's Tip: Make sure you are honest in whatever you list, as companies will verify education information.

If you are getting your next job based on your work experience and you graduated from high school only, you do not have to list your high school as that is a given on your resume. However, if you didn't graduate from high school and went back and earned a GED, it is important to list this accomplishment on your resume. This shows someone who is trying to better himself or herself and correct a deficiency and who is putting forth the extra effort to be able to compete in the job market.

Your degree, major, school, location, and dates should all go on one line. The following are examples of how to write the Education section.

EDUCATION
BS/Communications, NC State University, Raleigh, NC   1998
Graduated cum laude in 3 ½ years   GPA 3.2/4.0
Dean's List last 4 semesters   VP, Sigma Phi Epsilon Fraternity

 Hart's Tip: You do not have to say you were at a school from 1994 to 1998, only the year of graduation.

MBA, Duke University, Durham, NC   2005
BS/Electrical Engineering, Virginia Tech, Blacksburg, VA   2000
Worked and personally paid for all education expenses

AS/Cosmetology, Wake Technical Community College, Raleigh, NC   2002

3 years majoring in Computer Science at Elon University, Elon, NC

Earned GED at Johnson County Community College, Smithfield, NC   2005
Passed on first try   All classes at night while working 40 hours a week

BS/Accounting, University of North Carolina at Chapel Hill
Played 4 years of varsity basketball, captain last year
Tutored elementary children in reading for 2 summers

WHAT TO INCLUDE IN THE EDUCATION SECTION

Be selective in what you choose to include in your Education section. Show things that indicate your intelligence, effort expended, time used for work, and leadership activities. If you have been out of school for more than 10 years and getting your next job based on your work experience, the traits listed above don't have as much meaning and you need to decide if they are important enough to include.

If your education is recent, show the date of graduation. If you graduated more than 10 years ago, list the information, but leave the dates off as shown in the last example. There is no reason to change the calendar dates to years in your Work Experience section to eliminate the age factor and then show your old graduation dates in this section.

Apprenticeship experience
If you have been through an apprenticeship program for skills training, you need to include this on your resume. This hands-on learning experience could be the key element in getting an interview and the job you really want. This is not a degree program usually found in the Education section but an essential part of the training needed to open many doors for you.

Still working on a degree?
If you have not finished your degree or are returning to complete a degree, you need to show this on your resume. It could help you in competition for an interview and a job. Many advertised jobs show the need for a 4-year degree as a requirement. Sometimes the job requirement is listed as a 4-year degree or equivalent experience. You must be honest, as in all parts of your resume, when you show your education items. Here are two suggestions, depending on your situation, that will help you in your Education section.

If you didn't complete your degree but have work experience or non-credit training that would give you equivalency to the 4-year degree, you can show your education this way:

EDUCATION
Business major (2 years), name of school, location

Then let your information on training and experience make up the equivalent part.

If you return to school to finish your degree after being off for a while, you can show it this way:

EDUCATION
BS/Business Administration, name of school, location   (expected 2006)
AA/Business, name of school, location   1996

If you have been out of school for over 10 years, do not show the date of your AA degree.

Or, if you didn't get an associate degree, you could show it this way:

EDUCATION
BS/Business Administration, name of school, location   (expected 2006)
Business major (1½ years), name of school, location

WHAT TO INCLUDE IN THE EDUCATION SECTION

Some schools in certain states give credit towards a degree for work experience. You should check with the school you attended as this may provide some credits and you wouldn't have to take as many classes to get your degree. Many schools have on-line courses that you might take to complete your degree. Please check so you can eliminate that roadblock to your future.

If you are pursuing your targeted job as a result of your recent education, put the Education section directly below your Objective. If your next job is based on your work experience, place the Education section at the end of your resume. In either location, make your degree and major field of study **bold** if it supports your targeted job. Do not bold the school, its location, or dates if you use dates.

TAKE ACTION

Now, visualize what you want to say about your education to advertise yourself on your resume and use the section on the following page to write that part.

WHAT TO INCLUDE IN THE EDUCATION SECTION

HEADING

OBJECTIVE

WORK EXPERIENCE

COMPUTER SKILLS

EDUCATION

ACTIVITIES

HART'S REMINDERS

☐ Did you list your Education in the appropriate area of the resume?

Make Your Resume Talk Page-34

CHAPTER 8
ACTIVITIES ARE CRITICAL ON YOUR RESUME

I believe your Activities section is almost as important as your Work Experience to get you an interview. Many resume preparers are against this section, so let me tell you why I think it is essential. Activities show the chemistry of who you are outside of the workplace.

First, let me give you an example. I strongly suggested that a 40-year-old applicant put down Eagle Scout as one of his activities. He questioned me repeatedly, but I insisted and, although it had been 20 years ago, he finally added Eagle Scout.

Here's the e-mail message I received 2 weeks later:
"Thank you Mr. Hart for making me put Eagle Scout as one of my activities on my resume. When I went to the ABC Company for an interview, I found out that the interviewer had also been an Eagle Scout. He told me I was selected for the interview because of my experience and skills and also because I had been an Eagle Scout and that made me different. He knew the effort, discipline, and dedication that I had to exert to get that award. Not only did I get the interview, **I Got the Job!**"

 Use the word ACTIVITIES and not INTERESTS. Activities are what you are doing or have done; interests are just what you are thinking about doing or would like to do.

The Activities section must be honest and it doesn't take much space to include it. What you use shows something about the chemistry of who you are outside of work. Charity activities show you care about others. Sports activities could indicate you are in good physical condition and are a competitor. Individuals who participate in competitive sports train to be the best and they want to win and that is an activity that supports Sales jobs and any other job where being the best is needed. Activities that indicate the fitness of the person are helpful. Also, activities that show you are giving something back (charities and volunteering) indicate a caring person. Unusual items give the interviewer more to talk about to find out if you fit into their organization.

Do not put down so much information in your Activities section that there is nothing left to talk about. Space prevents that, but leave room for the questioning mind to ask and give you a chance to answer (and to show your oral communication skills).

ACTIVITIES ARE CRITICAL ON YOUR RESUME

You should not list religious or political activities unless that is your objective. If you are from a different religion or political party than the interviewer, it could affect your ability to get an interview and an offer. There are ways to work through such activities and still say something about you as a person and allow room for discussion. Look at these examples.

Activities (Before)	Activities (Revised)
Volunteer at Vacation Bible School	Mentor children
Teach Sunday School	Mentor children
Church choir	Musician
Handbell choir	Musician
Member of local political group	Fundraiser

You do not have to put down everything you've ever done in the Activities section. Write something that depicts who you really are and the nature of your character by the activities you are in or have been in. Showing three or four examples is enough. If you put down too many activities, a potential employer might think you don't have time to work.

Here are some activities that might show the chemistry of who you are:

CPR Certified
Habitat for Humanity
Soup kitchen volunteer
Run half marathons
Water aerobics
Competitive swimmer
Golf
Tennis
Interscholastic sports
EMT
Band
Tutor
Dancing
Licensed ham radio operator

ACTIVITIES ARE CRITICAL ON YOUR RESUME

Based on the last example, I'd like to share an e-mail quote from another person with whom I worked with on her resume.

"I found your class very enlightening and the guidelines in your book very practical. Now let me tell you the rest of the story. After revising my resume as explained in your book and meeting with you one-on-one, I put in my Activities section that I had been a licensed ham radio operator. I sent out a few resumes in response to vacancy announcements and soon got a call to come for an interview.

"The hiring manager said he selected me as one of the candidates to interview because of my experience in the IT industry but also because he couldn't believe a woman had been a licensed ham radio operator (one of his hobbies). I blew him away on my knowledge of ham radios and got the job. Not only did I get the job, but I have more responsibility than I've ever had, more people working for me, and making more than I've ever made in a very challenging and rewarding position. Thank you for making me put 'licensed ham radio operator' as an Activity on my resume."

There is no magic for things you include in your Activities section, and it won't work for everyone.

However, it could be the difference you need to get an interview.

What you say about your Activities and the chemistry of who you really are might be the items that open doors for you.

TAKE ACTION

Now, draft some of your past and present activities in the section provided and then be selective in what you decide to keep on your actual resume.

ACTIVITIES ARE CRITICAL ON YOUR RESUME

HEADING

OBJECTIVE

WORK EXPERIENCE

COMPUTER SKILLS

EDUCATION

ACTIVITIES

HART'S REMINDERS

☐ Did you list activities that indicate your chemistry and will not subject you to discrimination?

CHAPTER 9
WERE YOU IN MILITARY SERVICE ?

Showing your Military Service on a resume is essential if that is applicable for you. The write-up will be very simple unless you are going to get your next job based on your military work experience.

All resume reviewers have a different idea of what military service means to them. Basically, it means an individual who (1) is disciplined, (2) can follow orders or provide leadership, (3) knows the importance of support and teamwork, (4) has endurance and physical strength, and (5) has allegiance to the U.S. Because of the different feelings that exist about the military, there is no practical reason to write what you did in the military or what kind of discharge you got.

Saying you were honorably discharged is a given as only a few are released otherwise. A high rank would show leadership, but where you were stationed is not important. If the person doing the interviewing was in the military, the questions will come because of that commonality and no space can properly provide the information that will be exchanged with the interviewer.

Whether it is full-time military service, reserves, or the National Guard, it does belong on your resume. The government and some companies give extra credit for military service. One student told me they left military service off his resume because he was in Vietnam and was advised that companies looked negatively on Vietnam veterans. **That is not correct. Military service is military service and that is the possible key to open doors for you.**

This is all you need to say. List the branch of service and the years served.

MILITARY SERVICE
US Army   Brigadier General   1980-2005

or

MILITARY SERVICE
US Navy   4 years

The latter will be used if your calendar dates age you and your service was many years ago. Reserve or National Guard time should also be shown. For example,

MILITARY SERVICE
US Army Reserves   1986-2002   or   15+ years
US Army (Active)   1982-1986   or   4 years

WERE YOU IN MILITARY SERVICE?

TAKE ACTION

If you were in the military, write your information here.

HEADING

OBJECTIVE

WORK EXPERIENCE

COMPUTER SKILLS

EDUCATION

MILITARY SERVICE

ACTIVITIES

CHAPTER 10
OPTIONAL ITEMS ON A RESUME

I probably stand alone on what I consider optional items on a resume. These are a summary, a list of accomplishments, memberships, awards or honors, and licenses. Each is addressed below and why I think they are not essential items on an advertisement resume.

Summary

The problem I have with Summaries on a resume is that, no matter the length of the resume, many of the statements I have seen in a summary are not supported in the rest of the resume. For example, you will see statements like "results-oriented team player" and never find any results to go with the task statements and no evidence that the person was on a team. Many personal characteristics are usually included in a summary (i.e., great work ethic, multi-tasked, self-starter), but no support is shown for these statements in the rest of the resume. Lastly, many summaries will say that the person has excellent oral and written communication skills and a reviewer can't find that the person ever said anything or the resume has spelling and grammar mistakes. When this happens, a reviewer tends to not believe the other statements in the summary.

 Many summary statements that I have read are heavy with technical terms, and it is most difficult to determine what the person has really done and how good they are. Many other statements are loaded with "buzz words" but do not explain what the person has done in relation to those words. That is why I don't consider a Summary an essential part of the resume. Some of the information in the Summary should go in the Objective and some of the information would help if it is included in the cover letter.

Memberships

Memberships are not an essential part of your resume because it is hard to show whether you are just a member or an active member. If you are applying for a manager's position, showing you are an officer in an organization would be helpful. Any organization that you belong to is usually directly connected to your work and is expected and therefore does not make you any different than most other applicants. For some, listing memberships just fills the page up. That is why I say that Memberships are an optional item unless you are an officer and using that fact to support the targeted job.

Awards or honors

Most awards and honors are listed to show you have received an award for something, but nothing is written as to what you did to get the award or honor. Under a separate caption, just listing awards and honors has no benefit to you. The only exception would be for high school students or college graduates.

 If you tie your awards and honors into your work statements as a result, then your successes take on more meaning.

OPTIONAL ITEMS ON A RESUME

Licenses

Licenses that support your targeted job should appear right under your Objective. Licenses that do not support your Objective could go on the bottom of your resume to show you have something else that you have worked to get and could possibly make you a better candidate. Most licenses are job-specific, and anything outside of that area is certainly an optional item.

Certificates vs. Certifications

Many individuals get certificates for attending a training session and put this information on their resume. Just attending a training session does not help you on your resume. The question is "What did you learn in the training session that will help you on your job?" Therefore, listing certificates that you have received does not add to your resume effectiveness.

However, if you take courses and then take tests for certification, these certifications are valuable to you and need to be included on your resume. If the Certifications support your targeted Objective, they need to go right under the Objective.

Many resumes I have seen try to use certificates and certifications interchangeably and that is not correct. The big difference is that certifications are the result of tests passed. Certificates are received for attending or surviving a training course or seminar.

CHAPTER 11
REFERENCES

Your references are very important, but they are not part of your resume. References are a **given** and you need to include them on a separate sheet and keep them in your portfolio to take to the interview with you.

Who should you use for a reference? You need to use two people who can speak about your work effort, expertise, and work ethic. The third person should be a personal or character reference. Many times it is better not to use your supervisor as a reference because he or she knows your end results but may not know as much about your daily impact as a peer or subordinate. Select your references wisely and be sure to get their permission before you put them down as one of your references. It is your personal decision who to use that can help you the most. You do not have to use the same references on every job you apply for as someone else may be better for certain jobs.

When making your list of references, show the names and relationships (companies they work for and title), phone numbers and e-mail addresses where they can be contacted. The e-mail addresses are optional because you want the potential employer to talk directly to your references and e-mail is an impersonal way of finding out about you. The enthusiasm and inflection in your references' voices is important to you.

Print out your references using the same letterhead you use for your resume and cover letters.

REFERENCES

RICHARD A. HART

600 New Waverly Place, Cary, NC 27511   (919) 851-xxxx (h)   (919) 304-xxxx (c)   rahart@aol.com

References

John Smith – (Fellow supervisor at Spicer's for 5 years)
1234 18th Street
Cary, NC 27513
(919) 500-xxxx (home)

Abraham Bourque – (Peer at ABC Company for 10 years)
4321 Ace Avenue
Raleigh, NC 27520
(919) 720-xxxx (home)

Chris Martin – (Long time friend)
616 Delray Road
Garner, NC 27582
(919) 101-xxxx (home)

 It is better to use the references' home phone numbers as they will be out from under their companies' umbrella and might be able to talk about more than just when you worked and your job title. Get permission to use the home number and indicate "home" after showing their phone numbers.

 After you have an interview that went well, you should call your references immediately and let them know that they might be getting a call from Company XYZ. You should also give them some information about the areas that they need to support for you. This support will reinforce what was said during the interview discussion. The references will appreciate this heads-up call as it is tough to respond to an unexpected call.

 Did you complete a form allowing your previous company to release employment information about you?

 Do not use e-mail addresses on your Reference list. The potential employer needs to hear the enthusiasm and inflection in the reference's voice in response to specific questions rather than a cleverly written but sterile e-mail message.

CHAPTER 12
HIGH SCHOOLS STUDENTS NEED HELP TOO!

"I am a high school student and desperately need a summer job or part-time job during school to raise money for college or just to pay for costly activities. What can I put on my resume that will help me get an interview?"

This statement is heard all the time, nationwide. High school students are competing with older citizens who have ample time and with college students who get out of school earlier in the spring. Many high school students will also be competing with other high school students. With this dilemma, let's look at **some ways to make high school students' resumes talk for them.**

How can you write who you are on a resume and be different from your competitors? No two high school students are the same. High school students need to show as many of the following items that they can honestly support on their resumes to help them get interviews.

  a. Mental ability
  b. Leadership activities
  c. Activities that display energy
  d. Activities that show persistence
  e. Different languages they speak or understand
  f. Physical condition
  g. Computer skills and level of ability in each

Also, they need to be ready for a walk-in interview and be able to complete an application.

Now let's examine ways to state these items on a resume.

Mental ability

Under the Education section, you need to show your current GPA if it is over 3.0. For example, you could use the following example under the Education heading.

EDUCATION
Completed junior year at St. John's High School, Charlotte, NC
GPA 3.54/4.0   National Honor Society

If your GPA is under 3.0, do not state a grade point average and concentrate on the other factors that show leadership, energy, patience, persistence, and physical ability.

Leadership activities

Many jobs require a supervisor or someone to take charge. As a high school student, these opportunities are rare, but leadership experience is one way of differentiating you from your competitors. For example,

EDUCATION
St. John's High School, Charlotte, NC
President of Junior Class (400 students)   Captain of tennis team

HIGH SCHOOLS STUDENTS NEED HELP TOO!

Activities that display energy

What have you done that shows you have worked hard on a school project, fund-raising activity, or class assignment? There may be other students who worked on the same thing that you did, but your role and hands-on effort and energy may have been different and resulted in something different. For example,

EDUCATION
St. John's High School, Charlotte, NC
Designed and personally worked 20 hours on Homecoming float
Raised $200 on athletic fund raiser for pledges supporting dance marathon

Activities that show persistence

In addition to projects that show energy and effort, it helps if you show you have had to be persistent to complete a project. Include comments such as

EDUCATION
St. John's High School, Charlotte, NC
Worked 2 months on science fair project that was completed on time and won honorable mention in original research category.

Or

EDUCATION
St. John's High School, Charlotte, NC
Learned gymnastics stunts with no prior experience by practicing 2 hours every day that earned alternate spot on school team.

In this section, it is not always the accomplishment that is important but the fact that you showed effort and stick-to-itiveness to complete the effort you started. Most things that show persistence will be individual projects rather than being part of a team.

Different languages

If you speak more than one language or are conversational in a language other than English, this could be a key differentiator when you compete for many jobs. Fluent English is expected and any other languages you speak, read, or understand are added assets in getting an interview and a job. Jobs dealing with the public in any capacity could best be performed by someone who had experience in more than one language.

Your resume should say "Fluent in Spanish and English" if you have an American-sounding name. If otherwise (Nguyen, Li, Tran, Rodriquez), you would say "Fluent in English and Spanish [or Chinese]."

Even saying "conversational Spanish" (or whatever other language you have) would make you different and help you in competition for a job.

Another item that would help you is "Sign Language."

HIGH SCHOOLS STUDENTS NEED HELP TOO!

What is your physical condition?

For some jobs, physical fitness is a key factor and should be addressed on your resume. Jobs such as working for a moving company, in a warehouse, as a lifeguard, or anything requiring lifting would be done best by someone who is in good physical condition.

There are various ways to show this on a resume. For example,

"Play interscholastic soccer"
"Competed in track and field events for last 2 years"
"Played club basketball for 4 seasons"
"Swam breaststroke and backstroke on high school swim team"

These are only suggested examples and are not intended to be all-inclusive. You need to think what you have done in or out of school that will give a real indication of your physical condition.

What are your computer skills?

Many jobs require some use of the computer as part of your duties. Therefore, it is very important to show your level of ability on the computer. As a minimum, you need to show your knowledge or level of experience. For example, you could use this format:

COMPUTER SKILLS
Advanced in WORD, Excel, and PowerPoint
Intermediate in Outlook, Quicken, and the Internet
Knowledgeable in Visio and PageMaker
Keyboarding (60 wpm)

Some students will have more experience and knowledge than others and your level of ability or knowledge may differentiate you from your competitors. The important thing is to be honest in your self-evaluation of your level of ability. **Please do not fudge or lie on your level of ability.** Stating a level higher than what you really have achieved could cost you your job and be a problem for you for the rest of your working life.

 Stating your keyboard speed and accuracy is a matter that most resume writers don't think about. Please add this to your resume if your speed is more than 60 wpm.

HIGH SCHOOLS STUDENTS NEED HELP TOO!

Resume vs. an application

Many companies that hire high school students will not accept a resume but ask you to fill out their application. This is understandable because many students have no previous work experience and don't have much information to put on a resume. If you have considered all the items described previously in this chapter and you find that many sections are blank, you need to be sure you have documentation in your portfolio to support the information you will need to put on an application.

You need to have at least the following items in your portfolio when you go to a business to submit your resume or fill out an application. You do not have time to run back to your car or go home to get this information. You will need:

a. **Extra copies of your resume (at least 3)**
b. **Dates of previous work experience (starting and ending month, day, and year for every job)**
c. **Previous supervisors' names and phone numbers**
d. **Social security number and card**
e. **Work permit**
f. **Driver's license or passport or both**
g. **Reference list (at least 3 copies)**
h. **Counselors' or teachers' letters of recommendation**

What if?

What if you didn't graduate from high school or you didn't have superior grades? Everyone is not the same so use your positive attributes to move ahead.

If you did not graduate from high school, but later earned a GED, you need to put this on your resume. It could be better than a diploma that was gotten even with bad but passing grades. Earning a GED shows that you wanted to correct a deficiency in your education and you put forth the effort and extra time to go back and get it.

If you have not made good grades, you need to honestly put things on your resume that you have done that reflect energy, persistence, and effort and what you accomplished or skill you learned on each previous project or job. The suggestions made previously could serve as your guide.

Special skills

Sometimes you have developed special skills or passed certain tests that could be useful in helping you to get an interview and a job. For example,

a. **Passed American Red Cross life saving swim test**
b. **CPR certified**
c. **First aid certified**
d. **Apprenticeship program**

HIGH SCHOOLS STUDENTS NEED HELP TOO!

Work experience

Sometimes your previous jobs will give you work experience related to what you want to do the next summer or part-time while you're going to school. Be sure to not only show what you did but also how good you were. Include results in your work statements to show you deserve an interview. There is no magic to do this, but you must think about your results after you finish a job. I'd suggest starting a resume as soon as you can and update it and revise it when necessary. It is not too early to start now.

TAKE ACTION

Use the following page to draft your first resume.

HIGH SCHOOLS STUDENTS NEED HELP TOO!

HEADING

OBJECTIVE

WORK EXPERIENCE

COMPUTER SKILLS

EDUCATION

ACTIVITIES

CHAPTER 13
COLLEGE GRADUATES ARE IN THE MIDDLE

College graduates have recent education and some kind of expertise but not much experience. Therefore, their resumes need to provide some insight into who they really are and what characteristics they have that will fit into a company's culture.

Most college resumes are "fishing" resumes and are not tailored to specific jobs. College graduates normally use the "shotgun" approach and send their general resumes to as many companies as they can in hopes of someone finding something in the resume that might get them an interview. They usually pick a region of the country, do their research as to what type of people the company hires, and then send them out to see what happens. This approach will work for some, but I do not recommend it for most graduates.

I believe that college graduates still need to use the concept of building their resumes as outlined in this book. They still need a targeted Objective to show what job they are trying to get and direct the resume to specific companies. They also need to include more information about their college activities than just lists. If the graduate or college student has any kind of work experience, that experience needs to be directed to the job now targeted.

I know that college placement offices line up interviews and you will get interviews just on that basis. However, the resumes that you provide to the college placement office will be read by those interviewers, and those resumes need to be targeted to show your positive aspects prior to your interview. You want them to look forward to your coming for the interview.

Here are some suggestions that need to be considered as you build your resume. After these suggestions are some examples of "before and after" resumes that will give you more suggestions for how to write a resume that will get you positive reactions and better interviews.

Throughout the building process, you need to keep asking yourself, "What are my best skills, what experience do I have, and how good am I?" The answers to these questions need to show up on your resume as you write each section.

COLLEGE GRADUATES ARE IN THE MIDDLE

Target your Objective

You need to target your Objective to specific titled jobs and also to each company you send or take your resume. Then you need to emphasize your recent education and any skills or experience you have to support the job you are seeking. You need to write this Objective as what you have to offer not what you are seeking or just an historical listing. Make sure it is an "offering" statement. Here is an example of the different kinds of Objectives, **targeted** (offering) versus seeking or historical.

Targeted (Offering) Objective

Electrical Engineer with General Electric bringing recent EE degree, internship experience, and skills in instrumentation, computers, and electronics, plus a team player with a great work ethic.

Seeking Objective

Seeking a position as an Electrical Engineer where I can use my degree and internship experience and contribute to your company and advance in responsibility.

Historical objective

Electrical Engineer with a fitting education in electrical engineering and experience in electrical instrumentation, computers, and electronics.

The differences may seem subtle at first, but they are significantly different. The targeted Objective shows what experience and skills you have. Then it shows the skills you can offer to the company. The seeking Objective is the "fishing" type and shows the job you would like to have but not what you can bring to the job. The historical Objective shows what you have done but that may not fit the job you are applying for and doesn't show what you can offer a potential employer.

Education

Your education is the key to getting a real interview and an offer. How well you did in your classes is the first indication of your ability to do the job you are applying for. If you have over a 3.0 GPA, show that on your resume. If you do not have a 3.0 GPA, do not show your GPA on the resume. You will have to show other positive things to make up for that grade point average. There may be many reasons why you did not have a high GPA. Remember, your transcripts will go with you to an interview.

If you worked part-time or full-time while going to school full time, your grades are going to suffer some. If you played interscholastic sports and had to travel and were extremely tired from all the practices, your grades are going to suffer. Some students have to drive or commute an hour each day just to get to classes and this is time that you are unable to study. Such factors will naturally affect your grades, and these factors need to be shown on your resume. If any of these factors pertain to you and you still have a GPA over 3.0, then this also needs to be shown as you have done well against your competitors who did not have such distractions.

Other things that need to be shown under Education that will help you are some of the awards that you got and are based on your GPA. Items like Dean's List, graduated cum (magna, summa) laude, National Honor Society, or honorary departmental sororities or fraternities that have a high GPA as a requirement show your level of grade accomplishment. You would want to put more than one of these valuable items on your resume under the Education section if you have them as the reviewer might miss one of them. Your level of achievement is important to a potential employer.

Work experience or internship experience

If you have any work or internship experience, you definitely need to show it on the resume whether it is related to your targeted Objective or not. You can show it as Related Experience or Other Experience rather than just Work Experience as a side caption. The fact that you have worked and dealt with people and problems means something to a potential employer.

You need to use bulleted statements that lead in with an action verb to show what your task was and how well you accomplished that task. Do not just use key words; show what you did in relation to those key words and how well you performed the task. Just doing the task is one thing; how well you did the task will make you different from your competition (see Chapter 5).
It is not easy to write these statements, but thinking about or re-thinking the impact your work had and putting that into words on your resume will let the reviewer know that you have worked and made a difference to the team or group that you worked with. (See chapter 5 for tips for writing work statements.)

When you write the statements, please give an idea of your persistence in doing a job, the energy or effort you gave to the job, and the relationship you had with fellow workers to accomplish each task.

Do not write your bulleted statements as paragraphs! Use single statements that **can** stand alone. Do not refer to statements above or below the statement itself.

Computer skills

Almost every job today has some use of computers. Therefore, it helps the reviewer if you show your level of ability in each area regarding computers. If you only have a few computer skills, you can show them this way.

COMPUTER SKILLS
Excellent in WORD, Excel, PowerPoint, and Internet
Intermediate in PageMaker and PhotoShop
Knowledgeable in Quicken and Outlook

If you have many computer skills regarding systems, software, and hardware, I'd suggest you use a Technical Addendum and show a level of ability for each item. You could use a page 2 to your resume and set up the page as follows:

Name

TECHNICAL ADDENDUM

<u>Category or item</u>   <u>Experience level</u>   <u>Last time used</u>
(See chapter 6 for an example.)

Using this format would give reviewers a snapshot of your ability in the areas they need, plus an overall view of other areas where you might also be able to help the company. Whatever you do, please be honest in the level of ability that you put on the addendum.

COLLEGE GRADUATES ARE IN THE MIDDLE

<u>Activities</u>

You need to show the Activities you have been involved with while in school. You cannot show religious or political items. You do not have to state everything about the activity. Leave room for the interviewer to ask you some questions about your activities. The Activities section shows some of the chemistry of who you are, where you spend your time, and whether you were a leader or a member. Many times the activities will differentiate you from your competitors.

Here are some activities that indicate what you do outside of the classroom that will help you when reviewed by a potential employer:

- **Volunteer tutor at elementary school**
- **Scoutmaster**
- **Assistant coach of Little League team**
- **Candy striper**
- **Read for the blind at retirement home**
- **Run half marathons**
- **Water aerobics**
- **Dance instructor**
- **Horse trainer for cerebral palsy patients**

Following are some "before and after" college resumes with critiques of the "before" resumes to point out things that need to be changed to make them more effective and get you the needed interview.

TAKE ACTION

Use the forms after each section to write your college resume.

COLLEGE GRADUATES ARE IN THE MIDDLE

College Resume A Before Revisions

ANDREW BENJAMIN
andyben@hotmail.com

Local Address		Permanent Address
PO Box 18236		3740 Calico Road
Raleigh, NC 27605		Angier, NC 27382
(919) 847-XXXX		(919) 489-XXXX

OBJECTIVE
    Full-time position in Computer Engineering; interests in design and communication.

EDUCATION
    North Carolina State University, Raleigh, NC
    B.S., Computer Engineering, May 2005
    GPA: 2.89/4.0 major, 2.75/4.0 overall

    <u>Coursework:</u>
    Wireless Communication, Networking, Digital Signal Processing, Microprocessors and Digital Design, Linear Systems, Logic Design, Asic Design, Communication Engineering

    <u>Senior Design Project</u>
    Leader of team which performed measurement of imbalances in Wheatstone Bridge using DSP and Texas Instrument Evaluation Board (TMS320VC5402).

COMPUTER SKILLS
    Languages: C/C++, Verilog, HTML
    Operating Systems: Windows 95/98/NT/2000, and UNIX
    Tools: Matlab, Cadence, HSPICE, AutoCAD 14

EXPERIENCE
    Intern, Ericsson, Inc., Research Triangle Park, NC (Summer 2004)
- Member of Satellite Software Development Group.
- Designed software in C++ to search through files, found, and displayed name of special signals and numerical values on screen.
- Loaded flush program from PC into AMPS and GSM mobile phones.

Teaching Assistant, ECE Department, NC State University (Fall 2003)
- Helped individual students with questions concerning Fundamentals of Logic Design and circuits.

    Assistant Network Administrator, Park School, Durham, NC (Summer 2003)
- Installed Novell Netware client software and configured workstations.
- Set up applications for use by staff and students on Novell application server.
- Performed network wiring upgrades and maintenance.

Additional part-time jobs in retail and hotel industries during academic year to pay for college education. Developed communication, negotiation, and time management skills.

HONORS AND ACTIVITIES
- IEEE, served as membership chair 2004-2005
- Dean's list, 2 semesters
- Founder, campus Ultimate Frisbee Club, increased membership from 5 to 35
- Enjoy designing and assembling sound systems

Richard's Critique of College Resume A

- ✓ Eliminate solid line clear across the page under the Heading. It could prevent a computer scan in certain software.

- ✓ The Objective should be targeted and show the job, company, and the experience and skills the applicant can bring to the targeted job.

- ✓ Under Education, the school, degree, and major should all go on one line.

- ✓ The names of the courses are not as important as the skills the applicant learned and this should appear in the Computer Skills section.

- ✓ The Computer Skills shown need to indicate a level of ability for each to show the reviewer how good you are in each skill to compare to your competition.

- ✓ The bulleted statements in the Work Experience section are just statements of tasks and the reviewer has no idea what the applicant can bring to the position he or she is seeking.

- ✓ Dean's List and leadership positions in school organizations should go in the Education section.

ANDREW BENJAMIN

andyben@hotmail.com

Local Address
PO Box 18236
Raleigh, NC 27605
(919) 847-XXXX

Permanent Address
3740 Calico Road
Angier, NC 27382
(919) 489-XXXX

OBJECTIVE
Entry-level Computer Engineer with IBM bringing recent degree, internship experience, and skills in networking, wireless communication, and digital, logic, and ASIC design.

EDUCATION
BS/Computer Engineering, NC State University, Raleigh, NC　　　　　　　　2005
GPA 3.25/4.0 overall last 2 years　　　　Dean's list 2 times
Membership Chairman, IEEE

Team leader for a 4-week study that measured the imbalances in Wheatstone Bridge using DSP and Texas Instrument Evaluation Board that provided research results for professor to finish project.

COMPUTER SKILLS
Advanced in C/C++, UNIX, and AutoCAD 14
Intermediate in Verilog, Matlab, Cadence, and Windows 95/98/NT/2000
Knowledgeable in HTML and HSPICE

EXPERIENCE
Intern, Ericsson, Inc., Research Triangle Park, NC　　　　　　　　　　　　2004
- **Designed software that searched through files and found and displayed name of special signals and numerical values on screen.**
- Loaded flush program for PC into AMPS and GSM mobile phones that gained knowledge of how computers impacted the telecom industry.

Teaching Assistant, ECE Department, NC State University　　　　　　Fall 2003
Helped individual students with questions concerning Fundamentals of Logic Design and Circuits that resulted in paid tutor position in Department.

Assistant Network Administrator, Park School, Durham, NC　　　　Summer 2003
- Installed Novell Netware client software and configured workstations that resulted in well laid out computer lab for students.
- Set up applications for use by staff and students on Novell application server that provided greater access to resource materials.
- Performed network wiring upgrades and maintenance that resulted in no downtime during work period.

ACTIVITIES
Tutor
Ultimate Frisbee
Sound system designer

College Resume B Before Revisions

521 30th Street, Huntington, WV 25701
Phone (304) 949-XXXX   E-Mail jes521@aol.com

JOHN E. SMITHSON

OBJECTIVE

To obtain an Electrical Engineering or related position providing the opportunity to make a strong contribution to organizational goals through continued development of professional skills.

SUMMARY OF QUALIFICATIONS

- Plan and organize work efficiently, good follow through with careful attention to detail.
- Have obtained a sound theoretical background in electrical engineering fundamentals complemented with seven years of industrial experience.

EDUCATION

West Virginia University Institute of Technology   Montgomery, WV
Bachelor of Science in Electrical Engineering   May 2005
   Courses taken include:
      - Introduction to Microcontrollers   - Protective Relaying
      - Automatic Control Systems   - Power Systems

WORK EXPERIENCE

MJ&F Company   Huntington, WV   January 1999 to Present
Electrician
- Fundamental troubleshooting of 120V control circuits.
- Performed conduit mapping/routing and fittings and support.
- Obtained Working Knowledge of the Following:
    Power distribution low, medium, high through 34.5kV
    Substation/Distribution for mining and industry
    Phase/Ground fault protection
    Radial feed configurations
    Combinational/VFD 3 Phase 480V motor control up through 800Hp

Spike Electric   Mt. Airy, NC   March 1998 to December 1998
Lineman
- 3 Phase power line construction
- Installed service drops

SOFTWARE AND COMPUTER SKILLS

Programming Languages
- C++, (Basics of Assembly)
- Simulation Software
- JAVA, ETAP*, Matlab, ALTERA

Complete Power System Analysis was accomplished using ETAP software

Richard's Critique of College Resume B

✓ Name should go first in the Heading, and there is no reason to say phone or e-mail because nothing else looks like a phone number or e-mail address except the real thing.

✓ The Objective is a fishing Objective and filled with "motherhood and apple pie" phrases. You need to target the Objective.

✓ The Summary of Qualifications statements are not supported in the resume and make a reviewer wonder if they are really true statements.

✓ Under Education, put the degree and major first and bold it. Do not bold the school, location, or year (only use the year, not the month and year).

✓ You do not need to show the courses taken as recruiters or reviewers will know what courses are in a major in electrical engineering at your school.

✓ The bulleted statements in the Work Experience section are just statements of tasks, and the reviewer has no idea what the applicant can bring to the position he or she is seeking.

✓ Some of the experience is related to the position sought, but the resume doesn't indicate that.

✓ Some computer and software skills are listed, but the applicant needs to show the ability level in each one to make them meaningful.

✓ There is nothing in the resume to get a reviewer excited enough to interview the applicant.

✓ The resume includes no outside activities to show the applicant's chemistry.

JOHN E. SMITHSON
521 30th Street, Huntington, WV 25701   (304) 949-XXXX   jes521@aol.com

OBJECTIVE
Entry-level Electrical Engineer with General Electric bringing recent degree, 6 years of experience, and skills in electrical troubleshooting, power distribution, and power line construction plus excellent computer skills.

EDUCATION
BSEE, West Virginia University Institute of Technology, Montgomery, WV   2005

GPA 3.2/4.0   Graduated cum laude   Dean's List 4 times
Worked weekends all 4 years of school   Earned 100% of college expenses
Completed 100-hour case study on controlling temperatures in all school buildings on a 24/7 basis that school later used in contract negotiations.

RELATED EXPERIENCE
Electrician, MJ&F Company, Huntington   1999-Present
- **Troubleshot 120V control circuits that ensured continuous operation of systems checked.**
- Performed conduit mapping/routing and fittings and support that provided valuable assistance and time savings for supervisor.
- **Worked on various levels of power distribution for industrial companies that gained first-hand knowledge and a greater understanding of the inner workings of the system.**
- Gained knowledge of phase/ground fault protection and radial feed configurations that made it safer to operate around high voltage lines.

Lineman, Spike Electric, Mt. Airy, NC   1998
- Installed service drops and later helped complete all connections as part of 3 phase power line construction that resulted in receipt of the Rookie of the Year award.

SOFTWARE AND COMPUTER SKILLS
Advanced in C++ and ETAP
Intermediate in JAVA, Matlab, ALTERA, and WORD
Knowledgeable in PowerPoint, Excel, and the Internet

ACTIVITIES
Tutor
Eagle Scout
Extreme sports

College Resume C Before Revisions

DAVID L. JEFFREYS
Adljeff@yahoo.com

Present Address
NCSU, Box 8001
Raleigh, NC 27607
Phone (919) 512-XXXX

Permanent Address
624 Walnut Street
Wilmington, NC 28403
Phone (910) 678-XXXX

OBJECTIVE
Seeking a secondary teaching position in mathematics that will also provide opportunities for coaching and/or supervision of extracurricular activities

EDUCATION
North Carolina State University, Raleigh, NC
B.S. Mathematics Education
GPA 3.80/4.0, May 2005

TEACHING EXPERIENCE
Cary High School, Cary, NC   Jan. 2005-May 2005
Student Teacher
- Instructed students in Algebra I, Geometry, and Algebra II classes
- Initiated and developed math club for high achievers
- Volunteered to assist with varsity baseball team

Apex High School, Apex, NC   Aug. 2004-Dec. 2004
Volunteer Tutor
- Tutored six students in remedial math three days per week
- Developed individual lesson plans and instructional materials for each student

OTHER EXPERIENCE
North Carolina State University, Raleigh, NC   Aug. 2003- May 2004
Resident Advisor
- Initiated, planned and organized educational, cultural, social, safety, service, academic, and recreational programs for the residence hall.
- Utilized problem solving skills to mediate conflicts between residents.

Wrightsville Beach Tackle Shop, Wrightsville Beach, NC   May 2003- Aug 2003
Sales Associate
- Sold tackle equipment and bait to customers
- Repaired rod and reels for saltwater fishing
- Organized all displays of tackle equipment

COMPUTER SKILLS
MS Windows, MS Word, PowerPoint, Excel

HONORS/MEMBERSHIPS
Society of Undergraduate Mathematics (Vice President)
Pi Mu Epsilon, Mathematics Honor Society
Deans List
Intramural Football & Baseball

REFERENCES
Available upon request

Richard's Critique of College Resume C

✓ The word "phone" doesn't need to be shown as nothing looks like a phone number except a phone number.

✓ The Objective should be a targeted Objective and show the targeted job, the targeted company, and the experience and skills the applicant can bring to the targeted job.

✓ All of the Work Experience statements are just tasks. None of the statements show what was accomplished in the task.

✓ The statement "volunteered to assist with varsity baseball" doesn't say that he actually coached, only that he volunteered.

✓ The Computer Skills need to show the level of ability for each skill listed to help the reviewer decide if the applicant is good enough in the skills listed to get an interview.

✓ "References available upon request" is not needed as that is a "given."

✓ The resume includes no outside activities to show the applicant's chemistry.

✓ The resume includes information under Honors that should go under Education.

DAVID L. JEFFREYS
dljeff@yahoo.com

Present Address
NCSU, Box 8001
Raleigh, NC 27607
(919) 512-XXXX

Permanent Address
624 Walnut Street
Wilmington, NC 28403
(910) 678-XXXX

OBJECTIVE
Math Teacher/Coach at West Raleigh High School bringing recent degree (3.8 GPA) and excellent student teaching experience plus skills in tutoring, development of lesson plans, motivating students, and coaching baseball.

EDUCATION
BS/Mathematics Education, NC State University, Raleigh, NC   2005
GPA 3.80/4.0   Graduated summa cum laude   Dean's list 8 times
Mathematics Honor Society

RELATED EXPERIENCE
Student Teacher/ Volunteer Coach, Cary High School, Cary, NC   2005
- **Taught Algebra I, Geometry, and Algebra II classes that resulted in the preparation of daily lesson plans, oral and blackboard presentations, and respect gained after motivating students to excel.**
- Initiated and developed Math Club for high achievers that resulted in school winning competitive Math award against other high schools.
- **Served as volunteer assistant coach on varsity baseball team and emphasized and taught advanced fundamental skills that became a goal to attain for every player.**

Volunteer Tutor, Apex High School, Apex, NC   2003-2004
- **Tutored 6 students in remedial math 3 days per week that resulted in all students passing end of year tests.**
- Developed individual lesson plans and instructional materials for 6 students that resulted in working guidelines and reference points when problems arose.

OTHER EXPERIENCE
Resident Advisor, NC State University, Raleigh, NC   2003-2004
- Initiated, planned and organized educational, cultural, social, safety, service, academic, and recreational programs for the residence hall members that resulted in something available for each student and gained friendships.
- Utilized problem solving skills that mediated conflicts between residents.

Sales Associate, Wrightsville Beach Tackle Shop, Wrightsville Beach, NC 2003
- Sold tackle equipment and bait to customers and repaired rod and reels for saltwater fishing that resulted in happy and repeat customers.

COMPUTER SKILLS
Advanced in MS Windows and Excel   Intermediate in MS Word and PowerPoint

ACTIVITIES
Active sports   Tutor

College Resume D Before Revisions

EDWARD A. MOORE

2124 Teebox Drive Phone (301) 809-XXXX
Montgomery, MD 20882 E-mail emoore21@towson.edu

Objective Entry-level Information Technology position with a public company

Education 2002-Present Towson University Towson, MD
Computer Information Systems
- 3.00 GPA within Major
- Member of Towson University Men's Swim Team

Work Experience Summer 2001 Aardvark Swim & Sport Rockville, MD
Sales Associate
- Handle Sales Transactions
- Open and Close Store
- Helped Customers with questions

Summer 2002 Lakewood Country Club Rockville, MD
Lifeguard
- Watched over the lives of club members
- Played a role in customer relations on a daily basis

Summer 2003 Flower Hill Swim Team Gaithersburg, MD
Assistant Head Coach
- Coached a team of over 90 kids from ages 6-18 years old
- Create morning and afternoon workouts everyday
- Organized swimmers so they are on time for events in a meet

Summer 2004 Towson University Towson, MD
Lifeguard
- Watched over the lives of pool members
- Watched over the lives of Camp Bravo during swim lessons
- Played a role in customer relations on a daily basis

Summer 2004 Dulaney Swim Club Towson, MD
Lifeguard
- Watched over the lives of pool members
- Played a key role in customer relations on a daily basis

References Available upon Request

Richard's Critique of College Resume D

✓ The name needs to go above everything else on a resume and should be no larger than 14 pt font size.

✓ You do not need to write out the words "phone" and "e-mail" as it is just more information for the reviewer to read and nothing looks like a phone number except one and the same goes for an e-mail address.

✓ The Objective needs to be targeted and not shown as a "fishing" or "seeking" objective.

✓ The major, school, location, and dates should all go on one line.

✓ All of the dates should go to the far right as it is more important what you have done and how good you are than when you did the task.

✓ The job title, employer, location, and dates should all go on one line.

✓ The side captions should be ALL CAPS and bold.

✓ The body of the resume can start at the left margin rather than evenly after the longest side caption.

✓ All of the work statements are just tasks and there is nothing to show the applicant is any good. Results are desperately needed to show that the person deserves an interview.

✓ The resume includes no outside activities to show the applicant's chemistry.

✓ "References available upon request" is not needed as that is a "given."

EDWARD A. MOORE
2124 Teebox Drive, Montgomery, MD 20882   (301) 809-XXXX   emoore21@towson.edu

OBJECTIVE
Information Technology Intern with UPS bringing excellent skills in Microsoft Office and other software products plus website design abilities.

EDUCATION
Computer Information Systems major, Towson University, Towson, MD 2002-2005
3.0/4.0 GPA in major
Swims long distance freestyle and individual medley on University Men's Swim Team

- Led 4-person team in a semester-long systems development case study to lay out a complete IT system for a company with only a $200,000 IT budget that resulted in written and oral presentation reports that made recommendations and explained the hardware, software, and staff needed for the entire company.

- Provided expert knowledge personally to case study and used Microsoft Office suite and Visio that developed the analysis needed to document and make the recommendations.

WORK EXPERIENCE
Lifeguard, various MD locations   Summers 2002, 2003, 2004
- Ensured the safety of all swimmers and pool visitors by carefully observing movement in and around the pools.
- Developed customer relations by taking the time to answer any questions and provide advice on training for swimming that encouraged young, potential swimmers to get involved.

Sales Associate, Aardvark Swim & Sport, Rockville, MD   Summer 2001
- Handled sales transactions with courtesy that resulted in repeat customers.
- Opened and closed store that developed responsibility and the trust of employer.

COMPUTER SKILLS
Advanced in Excel, Word, PowerPoint, Outlook, FrontPage, and Internet
Intermediate in C++, HTML, and Windows 95/98/XP
Knowledgeable in Visio

ACTIVITIES
Golf
Competitive team sports
Guitar
Dogs

CHAPTER 14
CHANGING CAREERS? FLAVOR YOUR RESUME!

Flavor your resume if you are changing careers from your previous work experience. By flavoring, I mean to use the words of your prospective occupation that you can extract from your previous work experience.

This will be a tough project but will be worth the effort when you finish your new resume. Using the reverse-chronological obituary resume that contains your life's work history will provide nothing that generally fits your new job.

Here are my suggestions and approach to use for your new, targeted resume when making a career change.

1. Write down all the skills needed for the new job.

2. Look at your old experience and see if there are any facets of this experience that even vaguely address the new job.

3. Look at your education and training to see if anything matches the new job.

4. Write bulleted statements that include past tasks that meet your new need and use words of the new industry in writing a targeted resume. Don't forget that you must be honest in what you have done that might meet the requirements for the new job.

Your cover letter must also show that you are changing careers. Let the reviewer know this so they can make a decision whether your previous skills are transferable to the new position. Being open about the change you are making will give the potential employer a chance to give you an opportunity and that is all you want.

The best way to show what I mean by flavoring your resume for a career change is to look at a couple of examples of reverse-chronological resumes and a cover letter and how the resumes were changed to meet the requirements and language of a different career. The following pages show two "before and after" resumes of students who wanted or needed to change careers, and both show the flavoring that is needed to get your resume read and get you an interview.

CHANGING CAREERS? FLAVOR YOUR RESUME!

Changing Careers Resume A (Policeman/Textiles to Sales) Before Revisions

Thomas W. Mahoney 6000 Smith Rd., Raleigh, NC 27620
(919) 271-xxxx <u>twmahoney919@aol.com</u>

QUALIFICATIONS:

    Supervisory Skills /Experience   Community Interaction
    Quality Assurance   Commitment/Loyalty
    Organizational Development   Information Management

OBJECTIVE: An interesting sales position with a growing company that will enable me to utilize the wide range of skills and experience that I have accumulated throughout my career

EXPERIENCE: City of Raleigh Police Department   Raleigh, NC, Police Officer   1999-2005
- Rendered first aid at accidents and investigated causes and results of accident.
- Patrolled assigned beat on foot and in patrol car.
- Assisted subordinates and supervisors in identifying and resolving problems/crimes.
- Controlled traffic, prevented crime and the disturbance of the peace and arrested violators.
- Maintained records and produced reports for investigations.
- Collected and protected evidence at crime scenes.
- Received two-meritorious citations.

Weavexx   Wake Forest, NC
Supervisor   1991-1998
- Assisted workers in solving work-related problems.
- Studied production schedules and estimated worker-hour requirements for job completion.
- Interpreted company policies to workers and enforced safety regulations.
- Maintained time and production records.
- Estimated, requisitioned and inspected materials.
- Directed and managed staff of 25 full-time employees.

George C. Moore Co.   Edenton, NC
Weave Room Manager   1990-1991
- Assisted workers in solving work-related problems.
- Studied production schedules and estimated worker-hour requirements for job completion.
- Interpreted company policies to workers and enforced safety regulations.
- Maintained time and production records.
- Estimated, requisitioned and inspected materials.
- Directed and managed staff of 97 full-time employees.
- Mechanic as needed.

EDUCATION: Southeastern Massachusetts University   Dartmouth, MA
    B. S. Textile Technology   1987
    Northeastern University   Boston, MA
    Electrical Engineering   1982-1986

REFERENCES: Available Upon request

CHANGING CAREERS? FLAVOR YOUR RESUME!

Richard's Critique of Changing Careers Resume A

✓ Resume should be printed with an 11-or 12-pt font size, preferably 12.

✓ Qualifications statements are not all supported in the Work Experience statements.

✓ Objective should go right under the Heading. The Objective should be targeted to a specific job and not just to an interesting position.

✓ The Objective should be written in third person. The complete resume should be written in third person.

✓ The job title line should all go on one line.

✓ The experience needs to be flavored to the targeted job and not just an historical listing of tasks.

✓ There is nothing in the work statements that shows how good the applicant is.

✓ References, or a mention of their availability, do not go on a resume as they are a "given."

✓ The writer needs to add an Activities section to the resume to show the chemistry of the person outside of work.

CHANGING CAREERS? FLAVOR YOUR RESUME!

Changing Careers Resume A (Policeman/Textiles to Sales) After Revisions

THOMAS W. MAHONEY
6000 Smith Rd., Raleigh, NC 27620 (919) 271-xxxx twmahoney919@aol.com

OBJECTIVE
Outside Sales Person for the Best Door and Window Company bringing 13 years of experience and expert skills in judgment, socialization, persuasiveness, multi-tasking, and relationship building.

EXPERIENCE
Police Officer, City of Raleigh, Raleigh, NC 6 years
- **Worked closely with many different types of members of the community developing bonds for gathering needed information that solved problems, investigated crimes, and carried out difficult and dangerous tasks with positive and continued relationships.**
- **Used persuasion and social skills to interview and negotiate with victims and suspects that uncovered the causes and perpetrators of diverse criminal activity.**
- **Used good judgment that resulted in safe actions and solutions to dangerous situations as well as full documentation and accurate reports of all activities and investigations.**
- Performed multi-tasking out of necessity, driving safely at high speeds to emergency calls while reading and typing on the computer and listening and talking on the radio, all while formulating and coordinating a tactical, guide-lined approach that resulted in the safe handling of critical situations.

Supervisor, Weavexx Corp., Wake Forest, NC 7 years
- Used people skills that successfully directed and managed two production departments consisting of a staff of 25 full-time employees.
- Multi-tasking decreased down time and defects by 20% by working as full-time department mechanic and inspector as well as supervisor.
- **Used good judgment and increased production rates by over 25% by solving work-related problems and setting up production schedules that efficiently used equipment.**

Also worked as weave room manager, R&D engineer, machine shop fabricator, and automotive mechanic/parts store manager.

EDUCATION
BS/Textile Technology, Southeastern Massachusetts University, Dartmouth, MA
EE major, Northeastern University, Boston, MA

ACTIVITIES
Classic car restoration
Trap and target shooting
Darts
Music

CHANGING CAREERS? FLAVOR YOUR RESUME!

Sample Cover Letter for Changing Careers

THOMAS W. MAHONEY

6000 Smith Rd., Raleigh, NC 27620   (919) 271-xxxx   twmahoney919@aol.com

Date

Mr. Peter Previdi
Sales Director
Best Door and Window Company
PO Box 1234
Raleigh, NC 27617

Dear Mr. Previdi,

Enclosed is my resume for the Outside Sales Position that was advertised on your web site. Paul McMellon of your installation department recommended I apply because of the overall experience I have plus my tenacity to see a job to completion.

I want to continue my professional career but with a change to sales. I have 15+ years of experience in manufacturing and law enforcement where I built lasting relationships and provided excellent customer and community service. My ability to negotiate, solve problems, and persuade clients to listen and buy in to reason is excellent.

I am looking for you to give me an opportunity to show I can do a job for you in sales. I am hungry to prove that. I will call you on (10 days after the date of letter) to see if you have any questions about the information on my resume and to set up an interview.

Thanks,

Thomas W. Mahoney

Enclosure

CHANGING CAREERS? FLAVOR YOUR RESUME!

Changing Careers Resume B (Manufacturing to Clinical) Before Revisions

919-555-xxxx (evening) 919-286-xxxx (day)	**DAMIEN HAWKINS** dahawkins@aol.com	6123 Gamble Drive Raleigh, NC 27612

OBJECTIVE: Clinical Research Associate Assistant, Data Entry, or Document Technician with a Clinical Research Operation (CRO) firm while completing the Clinical Trials Research Associate (CTRA) program at Durham Technical Community College.

WORK EXPERIENCE:

Manufacturing / Quality Consultant, Raleigh, NC   2003 – present
- Investigated and solved quality problems with a design change that satisfied client's customer.
- Purchased material and built prototype mechanism that a venture partnership delivered to their customer for test.

Operations Manager, MetaControl Technologies, Morrisville, NC   2000 – 2002
- Delivered 1000 motor control modules to OEM customers within the first 12 months of operations of a start-up company by close collaboration with engineering, sales and key customers.
- Prepared and executed product release plans that expedited shipment of additional new products.
- Qualified prospective suppliers and implemented material planning and procurement processes that reduced risks on critical purchased parts.
- Managed budgets and schedules with contract manufacturers and engineering service firms.
- Analyzed inventory data and corrected variances that maintained record integrity.

Manufacturing Programs Manager, IBM, RTP, NC   1998 – 2000
- Introduced new network router into production on schedule through detailed project management of manufacturing activities at multiple remote locations.
- Communicated manufacturing status and issues on new products to IPT (Integrated Product Team) by effective and timely written and oral reports.
- Prevented production problems by conducting thorough manufacturing readiness reviews.

Manufacturing Manager, ATI Industrial Automation, Garner, NC   1996 – 1998
- Reorganized company's manufacturing operations that supported 10% sales growth in first fiscal year and 48% in the next (from $1.9 million to $3.2 million).
- Reduced cost of goods sold as a percentage of sales by implementing professional procurement practices for electronic and mechanical material, and improving production tools and processes.

New Product / Manufacturing / Procurement Engineer, IBM, RTP, NC   1984 – 1996
- Established a systematic process to improve the ease of manufacture of new PTH/SMT electronic assemblies during the design phase that was adopted as a model at other locations.
- Led change from internal to industry (IPC) design and documentation standards that shortened procurement cycles and reduced purchased material costs.
- Managed contract manufacturers worldwide implementing engineering changes and solving process problems that ensured a continuous supply of assemblies.

TRAINING:
- Computer: MS Office (strong), Excel (strong), MS Project (intermediate),
- Business   Project Management, Problem Solving, Managerial Cost Accounting, Negotiation
- Mfg   Six Sigma methods, ISO9000 Auditing, Certified Quality Auditor (CQA) – in process

EDUCATION and PROFESSIONAL:
- **MME** / Mechanical Engineering, NCSU, Raleigh, NC
- **BS** / Biology-Zoology, Duke University, Durham, NC
- **ASQ** (American Society for Quality), member
- **ACRP** (Association of Clinical Research Professionals), student member

ACTIVITIES:
- Supervised 12-20 volunteers over 14 Saturdays to construct a Habitat for Humanity Home.
- Served as Vice Chair on $3,200,000 building project from conception to occupancy.

CHANGING CAREERS? FLAVOR YOUR RESUME!

Richard's Critique of Changing Careers Resume B

✓ The Work Experience appears to have been written for a manufacturing job with no consideration that the applicant wants to change careers. The statements are well written but don't apply to the new direction for the applicant.

✓ The Objective is not supported by any of the Work Experience statements.

✓ Objective uses two abbreviations that are never used again. These abbreviations may be used as buzz words or key acronyms for computer scan purposes, but if the resume is selected based on the scan, nothing will materialize as the resume doesn't support any clinical technician skills.

✓ The Objective mentions three positions the applicant is seeking, but each job should be used in a different resume and the Work Experience tailored to each different job.

✓ The Objective contains no experience or skills to support the targeted job.

Author's Note – When reading the "after" resume notice how the Work Experience statements, based on actual work performed, have been flavored or changed to use skills that are used in the new industry and on the targeted job.

Changing Careers Resume B (Manufacturing to Clinical) After Revisions

DAMIEN HAWKINS

6123 Gamble Drive Raleigh, NC 27612 (919)-286-xxxx (day) (919)-555-xxxx (eve) dahawkins@aol.com

OBJECTIVE: Clinical Research Associate at IncResearch bringing 15 years of manufacturing and operations experience and skills in new product introduction, project management, quality and process control, planning, documentation, and meeting regulatory requirements.

EDUCATION:
- **AAS/Clinical Trial Research Associate**, Durham Technical CC, Durham, NC (target -2006)
- **Masters of Mechanical Engineering**, North Carolina State University, Raleigh, NC
- **BS/Biology/Zoology,** Duke University, Durham, NC

RELATED EXPERIENCE:
Project Management
- **Introduced new products on schedule through detailed project management of tasks at multiple remote locations including South America, Latin America, Europe and Far East.**

- **Prepared deadline driven project plans that identified dependencies, resources and risks that improved control over the project's critical path.**
- **Anticipated and avoided problems by conducting thorough phase entry readiness reviews.**
- Managed budgets and schedules with contractors and service firms that prevented cost overruns and delays.
- Communicated status and issues to interdisciplinary project teams and executive sponsors by effective and timely written and oral reports.
- Closed project files with a final report including "lessons learned" that improved performance on future projects.

Quality and Process Control
- **Ensured that project plans and control documents satisfied the requirements of domestic and international regulatory authorities by understanding their requirements.**
- **Trained suppliers in data collection then analyzed and investigated variances that maintained record integrity.**
- Implemented changes and solved process problems that ensured a continuous supply of product.
- Qualified prospective suppliers before awarding work that avoided performance problems.
- Wrote Statements of Work and ensured compliance by measuring and monitoring supplier performance including on-site visits.
- Implemented new or revised Standard Operating Procedures that established defined, repeatable and measurable processes.

WORK HISTORY:

Manufacturing and Quality Consultant, Raleigh, NC	2003 – present
Operations Manager, MetaControl Technologies, Morrisville, NC	2000 – 2002
Manufacturing Programs Manager, IBM, RTP, NC	1998 – 2000
Manufacturing Manager, ATI Industrial Automation, Garner, NC	1996 – 1998
Engineer - New Product / Manufacturing / Procurement, IBM, RTP, NC	1984 – 1996

ACTIVITIES:
Habitat for Humanity volunteer   Vice Chair on a 3-year $3.2 million building project

CHANGING CAREERS? FLAVOR YOUR RESUME!

DAMIEN HAWKINS

6123 Gamble Drive Raleigh, NC 27612   (919)-286-xxxx (day)   (919)-555-xxxx (eve)   dahawkins@aol.com

TECHNICAL ADDENDUM

Lab Course Work
Comparative Anatomy
Experimental Genetics
Inorganic and Organic Chemistry

Analysis and Communication Skills
Applied Statistics – intermediate
Mathematical Modeling of Mechanical Systems - advanced
Mathematical Modeling of Biological Systems - intermediate
Business Writing – advanced
Public Speaking – intermediate

Computer Skills
MS Excel – advanced
MS Word - intermediate
MS Project - intermediate

Business Training
Written Business Communication – North Carolina State University Industrial Extension Service
Principles of Marketing – North Carolina State University
Selling Skills for Professionals - IBM
Negotiation - IBM

Management Training
Management Accounting – North Carolina State University
Project Management in a Team Environment - IBM
Contract Management – IBM

Quality Training
ISO 9000-2000 Auditor Training - MetaControl
Applied Statistical Process Control - IBM
Design for Six Sigma - IBM

Leadership Training
Systematic Teamwork for Problem Solving, Decision Making, and Planning -IBM
Wilderness Leadership Course (28 days) – North Carolina Outward Bound School

Future Training Plans over next 12 months
Certified Quality Auditor, American Society for Quality
Project Management Professional, Project Management Institute

Professional Associations
Association of Clinical Research Professionals, student member
American Society for Quality, member

CHANGING CAREERS? FLAVOR YOUR RESUME!
NOTES

CHAPTER 15
RETURNING TO A JOB YOU USED TO DO

Have you ever thought about returning to a job you used to have? It may not be difficult if that job made you happy, and you still have the passion to do it.

One thing is certain. You will have to drastically change the format and organization on any resume you write to apply for a job that you used to do but haven't done for a while.

You will need to tailor your experience and skills to the job, but you must change the order of your jobs, and use years rather than calendar dates. It will be extremely hard to use the reverse-chronological order of jobs and calendar dates to get any attention on an advertisement resume. You will also need to target your Objective and then support the experience and skills in the Work Experience statements.

You will need to beef up your experience and skills of your former job that you want to return to, and downplay the amount you write about your other jobs. You will need to write results for all your bulleted statements to show how good you have been. You will also need to tailor your resume to the specific skills needed.

If you don't have a specific targeted job, you will need to go to the Internet and look up a job with the title you are hoping to get and tailor your resume to the skills and experience shown for that particular job. Do not write merely an historical resume loaded with bulleted statements that don't support your targeted Objective.

The next few pages will show a "before-and-after" resume, with a critique in between, to show how the resume must be written to be effective.

RETURNING TO A JOB YOU USED TO DO
Return-to Earlier-Job Resume Before Revisions

DIANE J. DONALD
3231 Elmwood Avenue, Cary, North Carolina 27513   (919) 564-xxxx

PROFILE

Effective and persuasive communicator offering strong interpersonal and presentation skills. Proven record of success in the cultivation of positive relationships with individuals at all levels. Areas of effectiveness include:

- Customer Relations
- Oral Communications
- Research/Problem Solving
- Administrative Support/Task Management
- Insurance Claims Management
- Accounts Payable & Receivable

➢ Welcome the challenges that are presented in settings that offer variety and provide opportunities to manage multiple tasks. Highly effective in environments where patience and the ability to provide direct assistance are crucial.

➢ Persistent and tenacious in the performance of research activities to solve problems. Able to initiate and maintain dialogues with key personnel to garner essential information.

PROFESSIONAL EXPERIENCE

Millennium Water LLC, Uncasville, Connecticut
Service Representative/Office Manager   2001-2005
➢ Hold concurrent responsibility for supporting account prospecting efforts and for managing business documentation for this contracting company providing well-water quality testing/analysis services to the commercial marketplace. Scope of office management responsibilities includes the processing of accounts payable/receivable as well as the preparation of outside correspondence.
➢ Follow up on prospecting leads and execute aggressive cold-calling strategies to introduce the company's services. Consistently effective in conducting presentations that highlight the benefits of comprehensive water testing and documentation-management programs to ensure alignment with state-mandated compliance protocols/guidelines.

University Medical Group, Providence, Rhode Island   1993-1996 and 2000-2001
Assistant Office Manager
➢ Utilized communication and interpersonal skills to facilitate daily office routines and support the delivery of comprehensive care for a six-physician surgical practice. Provided front-line patient relations and acted as an information resource to manage administrative matters, resolve third-party billing issues, and convey essential information, with a focus on meeting patients' needs and physician's obligations.
➢ Managed the scheduling function for all surgical and diagnostic procedures. Communicated directly with personnel at area hospitals and affiliated professional offices to coordinate schedules and confirm the availability of medical staff assisting with surgeries.
➢ Maintained hard-copy filing systems and set up patient profiles on a computer database. Performed medical transcription as needed to facilitate the management of medical records.
➢ Processed and submitted disability and insurance forms. Researched insurance eligibility guidelines and applied billing codes as necessary to expedite the forwarding of reimbursements.

RETURNING TO A JOB YOU USED TO DO

Estate Wood, Pascoag, Rhode Island 1997-2000
Independent Sales Representative
- Recognized and capitalized on the opportunity to represent a distinctive line of custom wooden flooring products serving the residential construction marketplace in the Nantucket, Massachusetts territory.
- Established a strategic alliance with a key distributor, rapidly acquired comprehensive product-line knowledge, and implemented aggressive account acquisition initiatives as the company's first-ever outside sales rep.
- Planned and conducted high-impact presentations to forge profitable relationships with area builders and subcontractors. Provided strong after-sale follow-up and support to develop a solid referral and repeat-clientele base.

Unemployed 1980-1993

Personal Assistant/Nanny 1972-1977
- Supported two different families and took care of the children
- Provided confidential work to help the career-minded adults continue to work
- Drove family members to all kinds of activities and worked business errands in with personal needs, but always prioritized the family needs first.

EDUCATION

Rhode Island College, Providence, Rhode Island
Completed almost two years of course work toward a bachelor's degree in business law.

Community College of Rhode Island, Warwick, Rhode Island
Completed course work toward an associate's degree in business law.

LICENSURE

Rhode Island Real Estate License

COMPUTER SKILLS

Working knowledge of Windows, Word, Medical Manager and the Internet

REFERENCES

Furnished upon request

RETURNING TO A JOB YOU USED TO DO
Richard's Critique of Return-to-Earlier-Job Resume

✓ Although the applicant wanted to be a Personal Assistant/Nanny, that isn't even mentioned in the Objective on the "before" resume. Using a Profile rather than an Objective is one of the reasons why this critical information is missing.

✓ It is impossible to write an effective resume to return to an earlier job if you use the reverse- chronological approach with calendar dates.

✓ Her resume uses great-sounding words, but still shows no positive results for any of the work performed.

✓ The resume is full of "to" statements indicating that the person did something positive. However, "to" statements state only what the person is supposed to do, not what he or she actually did. Use past-tense action verbs to show what you have done and how well you did it.

✓ "As needed" and "as necessary" also do not mean that you did anything. Avoid the use of these words and show what you really did.

✓ The resume is not tailored to any job and is basically an obituary resume written in an historical, reverse-chronological manner.

Author's note - See how the "after" resume changes to reflect earlier work and is tailored to the job the applicant really wants.

RETURNING TO A JOB YOU USED TO DO

Return – to – Earlier Job Resume After Revisions

DIANE J. DONALD
3231 Elmwood Avenue, Cary, NC 27513 (919) 564-xxxx

OBJECTIVE
Personal Assistant/Nanny with the Wright Family bringing 5 years of experience and skills in confidentiality and social areas that allowed families to live a successful and carefree life and the children to live in a safe and healthy environment.

RELATED EXPERIENCE
Personal Assistant/Companion, 2 RI families   5 years
- **Provided a safe, healthy, and positive environment and lifestyle to families with up to 4 children that allowed parents to continue careers and live successful, carefree lives.**
- Developed plans for dinner parties and contracted with vendors that resulted in successful events, many thanks, and welcomed guests.
- **Chauffeured family members and guests safely to appointments, airports, business meetings, and social gatherings plus ran errands that reduced stress and made life easier for the families.**

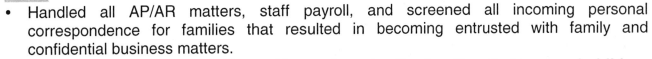

- Handled all AP/AR matters, staff payroll, and screened all incoming personal correspondence for families that resulted in becoming entrusted with family and confidential business matters.
- **Attended counseling sessions with teachers for the families that ensured children stayed on track and had no problems that were impacting their grades and advised parents of matters that needed their attention.**
- **Prioritized time with family members that still allowed time for marketing, errands, and recreation.**

OTHER EXPERIENCE
Assistant Office Manager, University Medical Group, Providence, RI   3 years
- Handled all office duties, learned the medical terminology, and solved many clients' problems without having to bother the physicians.
- Scheduled all surgeries and prepared all paperwork for insurance companies that resulted in excellent customer service.

Stay-at-Home Mom, Providence, RI   5+ years
- **Learned life skills in listening, time management, budgeting, negotiation, and problem solving that are present at every job performed.**

Also worked as a Sales Representative/Office Assistant for Millennium Water LLC in CT.

EDUCATION
AA/Business Law, Rhode Island Community College, Warwick, RI   (Expected 2006)
Earned GED and restored love of education

ACTIVITIES
CPR   Red Cross   Charity volunteer   Revolutionary and Civil War enthusiast

RETURNING TO A JOB YOU USED TO DO
NOTES

CHAPTER 16
TAILOR YOUR RESUME TO A SPECIFIC JOB

Tailoring your resume to a specific job is critical if you want to get an interview. What do you send to a person who says "Send me your resume and I will try to help you?" What you send will probably be an historical resume listing your past tasks. Such general resumes that are historical, reverse-chronological resumes are not the best way to get noticed. You need to find out something about the job so you can describe your skills and ability to perform for a new employer. With all the competition for jobs, you must get the attention of the reader in the 30-second time of review.

There is no magic to do this. One way to help would be to use "Related Experience" and "Other Experience" instead of Work Experience as side captions and this would put the support you need right under your Objective. It would also meet the "Rule of Thumb" criteria. You will need to get the reverse-chronological thoughts out of your head and think what you have done to best support the job you are applying for.

To explain what I mean by tailoring your resume to a specific job, I am going to show you a general resume I received that was used to apply for two completely different jobs. Then I am going to show the resumes that were tailored for each of the jobs.

TAILOR YOUR RESUME TO A SPECIFIC JOB

General Resume for Two Different Jobs Before Revisions

MICKEY SPRINGSTEEN
92 Pinehurst Drive, Hurricane, WV 25526   (304) 757-XXXX

OBJECTIVE: To coach college football or teach in high school

EDUCATION: Masters of Arts, Special Education
　University of New Mexico, Albuquerque, NM (1989)
Graduate Course Work
　Capital University, Bexley, OH (1985-1986)
Graduate Course Work
　Marshall University, Huntington, WV (1984-1985)
Bachelor of Arts, Physical Education and Driver's Education
　West Virginia Tech, Montgomery, WV (1982)

COACHING EXPERIENCE

Head Football Coach, 2003-2004
University of Charleston, Charleston, WV 25304
First year (2003) for football in over 50 years
Record 7-13

Head Football Coach, 1999-2003
West Virginia Tech, Montgomery, WV 25136
Record 17-27
Record vs. NCAA Division II 17-18

Offensive Coordinator, 1996-1997
Homewood-Flossmoor High School, Flossmoor, IL 60422
Team Record 8-4, State Quarter Finals

Head Coach, 1994-1995
Thornridge High School, Dolton, IL 60419
Record 9-9

Offensive Skills Coach, 1993
Homewood-Flossmoor High School, Flossmoor, IL 60422
Team Record 9-1

Offensive Coordinator, 1992
Concord College, Athens, WV 24712
Team Record 7-3-1

Offensive Coordinator, 1991
Glenville State College, Glenville, WV 26351
Team Record 5-4-1

TAILOR YOUR RESUME TO A SPECIFIC JOB

Offensive Coordinator, 1990
West Virginia Tech, Montgomery, WV 25136
Team Record 3-7

Offensive Backs, Special Teams, Volunteer Assistant, 1989
UTEP, El Paso, TX 79968
Team Record 2-10

TEACHING EXPERIENCE

Supervisor C.A.R.E. Unit (Discipline), 1993-1999
Thornridge High School, Dolton, IL 60419

Special Education LD-BD, 1993
Eisenhower Elementary School, South Holland, IL 60473

PE Instructor, 1992
Concord College, Athens, WV 24712

Supervisor, Student Teaching, 1991
Glenville State College, Glenville, WV 26351

PE Instructor, 1990
West Virginia Tech, Montgomery, WV 25136

Special Education LD, 1989
Eastwood Middle School, El Paso, TX 79968

Special Education Instructor, 1988
MacArthur Elementary School, Albuquerque, NM 78111

REFERENCES

Harry Smith
Head Football, Coach, Homewood-Flossmoor HS, Flossmoor, IL
(708) 799-XXXX

Jess Lilly
Head Football Coach, Glenville State College, Glenville, WV 26351
(304) 581-XXXX

Dr. Peter Kelley
President, West Virginia Tech, Montgomery, WV 25136
(304) 442-XXXX

Richard's Critique of General Resume, not Tailored

✓ **No statements in this resume describe what the person really did and how good he was. Lists of information do not excite a reader to want to interview this applicant. With both coaching and teaching listed, we do not know what the person really wants to do now. Even with the lists on this resume, items like zip codes and references are not needed. Please observe how this person changed his resume when it was tailored to two different jobs that the person was really qualified to do.**

TAILOR YOUR RESUME TO A SPECIFIC JOB

Tailored Resume for Coaching Job After Revisions

MICKEY SPRINGSTEEN
92 Pinehurst Drive, Hurricane, WV25526   (304) 757-XXXX

OBJECTIVE
Head Football Coach at Weldon College bringing 14 years experience, including 5 years of NCAA Division II head-coaching experience, and creative skills for offenses and hard-nosed skills for defenses.

RELATED EXPERIENCE
- **Inherited a program that had won 6 games in 10 years and improved it into a team with winning records in 3rd and 4th years.**
- **Worked closely with administrators, faculty, and staff to improve football program, but kept it in perspective with academics to provide a balanced program for the entire school that was appreciated by the students and alumni.**
- Recruited student/athletes locally and nationwide after working with selected players and parents to sell the football and academic programs of the university, and continued to support them throughout their careers.
- **Developed technical offensive and defensive skills for all positions that built programs into competitive status and still made it fun for all participants.**
- Initiated tutorial program that improved the graduation rate and grade point averages for entire team.
- Initiated and provided all start-up duties for a university's football program that had been dormant for over 50 years, and built it into a competitive team in first year.
- Acquired defensive skills through development of schemes to stop various offenses that resulted in victories.

COLLEGE COACHING HISTORY
Head Football Coach, University of Charleston, Charleston, WV	2003-Present
Head Football Coach/AD, West Virginia Tech, Montgomery, WV	1999-2003
Offensive Coordinator, Concord College, Athens, WV	1992
Offensive Coordinator, Glenville State College, Glenville, WV	1991
Offensive Coordinator, West Virginia Tech, Montgomery, WV	1990
Special Teams/Backfield Coach, UTEP, El Paso, TX	1989

OTHER EXPERIENCE
- Taught and supervised special education classes that changed the future for many students as they began to participate in regular classes and learn daily how to behave and learn.

EDUCATION
MA/Special Education, University of New Mexico, Albuquerque, NM	1989
Graduate Course Work/Health, Capital University, Bexley, OH	1985-1986
Graduate Course Work/Safety Ed, Marshall University, Huntington, WV	1984-1985
BA/PE and Driver's Ed, West Virginia Tech, Montgomery, WV	1982

ACTIVITIES
Golf   FCA   Ordained Minister

MICKEY SPRINGSTEEN
92 Pinehurst Drive, Hurricane, WV 25526   (304) 757-xxxx

COACHING AND TEACHING ADDENDUM

Other Football Coaching Experience

Offensive Coordinator, Homewood-Floosmoor HS, Floosmoor, IL	1996-1997
Head Football Coach, Thornridge HS, Dolton, IL	1994-1995
Offensive Skill Position Coach, Homewood-Floosmoor HS, Floosmoor, FL	1993

Teaching Experience

Supervisor C.A.R.E. Unit (Discipline) Thornridge, HS, Dolton, IL	1993-1999
Special Education LD-BD, Eisenhower Elementary, South Holland, IL	1993
PE Instructor, Concord College, Athens, WV	1992
Supervisor, Student Teaching, Glenville State College, Glenville, WV	1991
PE Instructor, West Virginia Tech, Montgomery, WV	1990-1991
Special Education LD, Eastwood Middle School, El Paso, TX	1989-1990
Special Education, MacArthur Elementary School, Albuquerque, NM	1988-1989

Football Clinic Instructor

Coaching the No-Huddle Offense, Randolph Macon Camp, Ashland, VA	2004
Tips for Using the Spread Offense, Capitol High School, Charleston, WV	2003
The Importance of Teaching Defensive Skills, Weldon College, Weldon, NC	2002
How to Mix Football with Academics, Evans College, Evans, WV	2001

TAILOR YOUR RESUME TO A SPECIFIC JOB

Tailored Resume for Special Education Instructor After Revisions

MICKEY SPRINGSTEEN
92 Pinehurst Drive, Hurricane, WV 25526   (304) 757-xxxx

OBJECTIVE
Special Education instructor at Holly Springs High School bringing 10 years experience and skills in listening, counseling, and working with students and parents that meet day-to-day challenges of each individual student.

RELATED TEACHING EXPERIENCE
- Counseled challenged students daily and worked personally with the most difficult ones with the result that no students were dismissed for behavior problems.
- **Supervised classes in the inner city with an annual average of 470 learning and behaviorally challenged students with the result that only 6% had to repeat classes.**
- Created learning centers that were named after local professional athletes/notables by the students that rewarded the students immediately after completing their task with the opportunity to accomplish a skill related to the star's profession.
- **Was assigned with a class of 4th and 5th grader LD-BD students and patiently worked with each that resulted in 3 students moving to the honor roll by year's end.**
- Used purposeful tasks learned in graduate school, and made little revisions to fit special needs, that increased student's willingness to change and improve their abilities.
- Developed lesson plans for various education classes that resulted in well-organized classes and students prepared to carry those plans to fruition when they started teaching.

Teaching Experience
Supervisor C.A.R.E. Unit (Discipline) Thornridge, HS, Dolton, IL	6 years
Special Education LD-BD, Eisenhower Elementary, South Holland, IL	1 year
Special Education LD, Eastwood Middle School, El Paso, TX	1 year
Special Education, MacArthur Elementary School, Albuquerque, NM	2 years
PE Instructor, Concord College, Athens, WV	1 year
Supervisor, Student Teaching, Glenville State College, Glenville, WV	1 year
PE Instructor, West Virginia Tech, Montgomery, WV	2 years

OTHER EXPERIENCE
- Coached high school and college football in TX, IL, and WV and built competitive programs at both levels, plus made academics a part of the recruiting and athletic program.

EDUCATION
MA/Special Education, University of New Mexico, Albuquerque, NM	1989
Graduate Course Work/Health, Capital University, Bexley, OH	1985-1986
Graduate Course Work/Safety Ed, Marshall University, Huntington, WV	1984-1985
BA/PE and Driver's Ed, West Virginia Tech, Montgomery, WV	1982

ACTIVITIES
Golf
FCA
Ordained Minister

CHAPTER 17

BONUS: SHORT, ACTION COVER LETTERS

Many times cover letters with a resume are as important as the resume. It includes the resume as an enclosure but is a separate advertisement of what you have to offer a potential employer written in first person. **Many students have said that cover letters don't get read and my only comment is, "Bad cover letters DON'T get read."**

 Cover letters are a separate advertisement from a resume and must show what you have to offer a potential employer and how good you are.

Cover letters should be short and properly set the scene as to the job you are applying for, where you found the vacancy listing to give the employer feedback on which ads are getting to prospective employees, and what you have to offer for that targeted position.

Every cover letter will be different because the applicants and their skills are different. You do not need to write your life history in a cover letter, but you need to put the important things to get a reviewer to keep reading so you can get an interview.

 Before you write the letter, try to get the name of the right person as the addressee. This may take some work (computer search or a phone call), but it is certainly worth the effort.

Here are the basics.

First paragraph of the cover letter

Always state the job you are applying for in case the company has similar or more than one vacancy listed. State where you found the vacancy announcement as that gives the company feedback on where to advertise vacancies in the future. If you heard about the vacancy from someone who works at that company or someone who has had positive contacts with the company, state that person's name and a comment from that person. This could start a chain reaction to get you an interview.

Please don't say, "As shown on my resume" as the cover letter and resume are two separate advertisements and must be stand-alone documents. The cover letter is a more personal document and includes personal characteristics while the resume is a factual presentation of your experience, skills, and results.

Paragraph 2 and/or 3 of the cover letter

This is your "bragging-rights" area where you compare your experience and skills to the skills required or preferred for the job that were stated in the vacancy announcement. Give a concrete and real example to nail down the first skill you list. You need to address four or five of the skills needed by the company.

BONUS: SHORT, ACTION COVER LETTERS

The reason that I say paragraph 2 and/or 3 is that you do not want a 20-line paragraph. It won't all get read. If you make it two 8- or 10-line paragraphs, you have a better chance of getting the reviewer to read more about your skills.

If the vacancy announcement lists many required experiences and skills, it would be better to use a split-page presentation that compares "your qualifications" to the "job requirements." If a split-page presentation is used, it becomes page 2 of your cover letter and a reference to it has to appear in paragraph 2 (see page 93). By making this comparison, you have done the reviewer a favor, and this could be the advantage you need to get an interview.

Last paragraph of the cover letter

The last paragraph is the action paragraph. You have to look out for yourself; don't sit at home waiting for your phone to ring. You must show what you are going to do and when you are going to do it. With the number of resumes received for any one job, Human Resources officers do not have time nor do they want to call all applicants. You must take the initiative and be sure you do what you say your action will be.

How do I handle the salary questions?

If you are asked to provide your salary requirements, you must provide this information in your cover letter. You would add a paragraph before your last, action paragraph and state at least a range of the salary you would require. "My salary requirement would be in the range of $38,000 to $45,000, and with my experience, I believe I should be in the high side of that range. We can discuss this in more detail during the interview." If the information is not provided, your letter and enclosed resume will not be considered.

If a salary history is required, you must provide it. It becomes page 2 of your cover letter, and you must have a reference to that effect in your cover letter. The format should be in reverse-chronological order and be in the format of your industry – annually or hourly. You can show it by title and company with a starting and ending salary or year by year. You need to provide information on the last 15 years. Here is one way to show salary history:

Peter A. Smith Salary History

Job Title	Company	Time Period	Salary
Project Manager	Goebel Enterprises	1999-2005	$72,000-$90,000
Senior Systems Analyst	Campbell & Ferrera, Inc.	1996-1999	$61,000-$71,000
Systems Analyst	Gold, Zimmer and Brady	1993-1996	$52,000-$60,000
Software Engineer	Elliott Technologies	1990-1992	$45,000-$50,000

Salary requirements and salary history do not go on a resume. They are addressed only in the cover letter. You might want to footnote an unusual year's salary that is out of line with the year before and after it.

Changing careers/returning to the workforce

If you are changing careers or returning to the workforce after being off for a few years, you need to address this factor in the cover letter. "I am returning to work after 10 years as a stay-at-home mom where I developed life skills in listening, problem solving, negotiation, organization, and budgeting. I also provided home schooling and updated my computer skills by taking four classes at Wake Technical Community College in Word, PowerPoint, Excel, and Quicken, plus earned a certification in the Administrative Professional Program."

BONUS: SHORT, ACTION COVER LETTERS

By mentioning these factors in your cover letter, you are making the employer honestly aware of your situation, and they will have to make a decision whether you fit into their employment plans.

The employer makes the decisions about who to interview, and your honesty in your cover letter and resume could be the difference in competition with other applicants.

Many students have said that they don't think employers read cover letters, but I believe you need to provide a cover letter with your resume and make it a separate and personal advertisement of how your skills and experience match the requirements for each job applied for.

The next three pages contain samples of cover letters and should give you an idea of what is recommended.

BONUS: SHORT, ACTION COVER LETTERS

Example of cover letter

Date

Richard A. Hart
PO Box 563
Holly Springs, NC 27540

Mr. Clyde Crewey
ABC Sports Sales Company
PO Box 1000
Raleigh, NC 27555

Dear Mr. Crewey,

Enclosed is my resume for the Sales Manager position that was posted on your web site. Bob Watson of your Industrial Management Department recommended that I apply because of my excellent sales experience in the sports equipment industry.

I have exceeded my sales quotas every year for the past 10 years. For example, my sales last year were 25% over my designated quota. This was not happenstance. I was able to keep all my customers from the previous year, plus add at least 2 new customers every month. This was accomplished by researching potential customers, setting up informal meetings, prospecting in a friendly and personal way, and then showing the potential clients the quality of all of our sports equipment. Most of my prospects were former athletes like me, and this relationship quickly formed a bond that grew to having satisfied customers.

For the prospects that were not from an athletic background but carried sports equipment in their inventory, I spent considerable time going over the quality and safety of our equipment. The time spent doing this paid off with new contracts and purchase orders. I can bring these same skills and traits to you and help you get a share of the sports equipment sales in and out of your immediate area.

I will call you on [10 days after the date on the letter] to see if you have any questions about my resume and to set up an interview.

Thank you,

Richard A. Hart

Enclosure

BONUS: SHORT, ACTION COVER LETTERS

Example of Cover Letter
with Split-page Comparison of Qualifications vs. Job Requirements

Juan Rodriquez
PO Box 1234, Raleigh, NC 27444   (919) 234-xxxx   rodriquezj100@aol.com

Date

Mr. Mervin McNear
McNear & Horne, CPA's
PO Box 987
Cary, NC 27333

Dear Mr. McNear,

Enclosed is my resume for the Accounting Manager position that was posted on Qualityjobs.com. One of your consultants, Tom Wilson of Hitt Advisors, also informed me of your opening and thought my experience and skills would be a good match.

I have attached a page that compares my qualifications to your job requirements. For each requirement, you will see that I meet or exceed your needs.

I will call you on [10 days after the date on the letter] to see if you have any questions about my qualifications and to set up an interview.

Thanks,

Juan Rodriquez

Enclosure

BONUS: SHORT, ACTION COVER LETTERS

Juan Rodriquez
PO Box 1234, Raleigh, NC 27444   (919) 234-xxxx   rodriquezj100@aol.com

Comparison of qualifications to job requirements

Job Requirements	My Qualifications
1. 4-yr. degree in related field	MBA from North Carolina State University BS/Accounting from James Madison University
2. CPA experience	10 years of experience with Campbell and Zimmer, CPAs where I worked on audits of many corporations and produced financial statements and annual reports with unqualified opinions. I found some errors that were corrected by the corporations to earn the positive opinions.
3. Knowledge of GAAP	I live by the yellow book and its requirements and apply GAAP requirements in all my work in the accounting and auditing field.
4. Management experience	I have 3 years of experience managing a 10-person office for Campbell and Zimmer. I have supervised diverse accounting and auditing staffs for 2-8 persons for the past 8 years and provided monitoring and OJT continuously that resulted in the promotion of subordinates and 100% retention of all assigned staff.

CHAPTER 18
PHYSICAL ATTRIBUTES OF A RESUME

Many things have to be considered to have an attractive, well-formatted resume. Items such as paper type and color, font type and size, margins, and spacing are important factors in preparing a resume.

Paper type and color

Use a white or off-white color paper of a weight a little heavier than normal typing paper. Use black type on the entire resume. Many times an e-mail address will appear as blue when viewed in your word processing software. To change this address to black type, highlight the complete blue address and go to the toolbar and click on the heavy black A and this will change the blue print to black print.

In considering the type of paper, you must realize that if additional copies are made for concurrent review, some readers are looking at your resume on cheap copy paper.

I have seen everything from pink and blue to laminated resumes, but the information on the resume is what gets you the interview, not the color or type of paper.

Font type and size

Use a font type that is easy to read – Arial or Times Roman. Once selected, use the same font type on the entire resume. Do not use italics as it is hard to read.

The entire resume should be in 12-pt font with two exceptions. The name can be 14-pt font and the rest of the heading (address, phone number, and e-mail address) can be as small as 8-pt font if a two-line heading is used.

Other necessary considerations for an effective resume

The resume must pass the 30-second test. The 30-second test is the time a reader gives a resume in a first (and maybe only) look to see if there is something that catches his/her attention to read more.

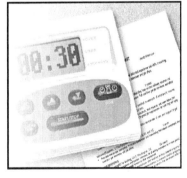

In addition to a font type that is easy to read, the resume should not be loaded with technical terms, acronyms, or jargon. Simple language is better than complicated words.

You must make good use of white space, and the typing should not crowd the margins (top, bottom, or sides). Use 1-inch margins for the top, bottom, and both sides. If you use full justification, be aware it may put extra spaces and gaps in the even flow of reading the resume and readers are not used to reading through gaps. Yes, it may look good to have exact 1-inch margins on each side, but it is sometimes easier to read if full justification is not used.

PHYSICAL ATTRIBUTES OF A RESUME

Some things need to jump out at readers to direct their eyes to what you want them to know about you in 30 seconds. **Make the following things bold type:**

1- **Name** (but not the rest of your Heading).
2- **The entire Objective (headline).**
3- **Certifications.**
4- **Job titles that support your Objective in your Work Experience section.**
5- **Two or three complete statements that best support your targeted Objective and describe your skills and successes.** If you use bold too much, nothing jumps out at the reader.
6- **Degrees and majors that support your targeted Objective.**

There can be no mistakes on the resume - spelling, grammar, or punctuation. Consistency in punctuation is also important and shows good organization. For example, if you use a period at the end of your Objective, put a period after each of your work statements. If you do not put a period after your Objective statement, then don't put a period after your work statements.

One of the biggest reasons potential employers throw out a resume is that it contains mistakes. The most common sources of mistakes are those "last-minute edits" when rushed to meet a deadline.

 Do not rely on spell-check to find your mistakes. For example, I have seen "Supervisory manger" on many resumes, but spell-check will not find that misspelling. When you do your own proofing, please read from a hard copy of the resume, not on the computer screen. It is a fact that 70% more mistakes are found when reading a hard copy than from reading the same material on a computer screen.

Your format must be attractive and consistent. **Ugly resumes won't get read.** For example, resumes written in 8 or lesser point font won't get read. Neither will resumes that have information in multiple boxes about the various jobs they think they are qualified for on one resume. Neither will resumes with narrow margins on all sides in small size font, as it usually gets this reaction: "Here comes the applicant's life history of tasks in 8-pt font."

Be very careful of the use of abbreviations. If not explained, they might mean different things to different reviewers. Review all abbreviations to be sure they are needed. Sometimes they are never used a second time and are thrown in as an unnecessary "key word."

Do not use "&" to save space. It only saves you two digits and you will find that the reviewer is counting them rather than saying "and." Only use "&" when it is part of the name of a company or P&L or R&D. Do not use it instead of "and" in a statement.

Do not use "etc." as the reader doesn't know whether you are really through or you don't know when to quit. It implies that you have more information to state when you might not have any. Therefore, don't use "etc." on your resume.

PHYSICAL ATTRIBUTES OF A RESUME
Hints to get to a one-page advertisement resume

1. Use a two-line Heading.
2. Use 8-pt font spaces (rather than 12) between sections on the resume.
3. Use one line to show job title (**bold**), company, location and dates (years).
4. Use one line to show degree and major (both **bold**), school, location, and year graduated (if used).
5. Leave off "References Available upon Request" (a given).
6. Use job specifics that advertise your skills and experiences and leave off the rest of your life history.
7. Show only the last 12-15 years of your work experience.
8. Do not include anything personal (religion, politics, height, weight, age, marital status, or children).
9. Use 1-inch margins on the sides, top, and bottom of the page.
10. Start all of your data 3 spaces in from the left edge of your section headings.
11. Shorter is better if it describes what you really did and how good you are.
12. Use only 8-12 well-written work statements with results to advertise your ability.

TAKE ACTION

Your resume should be reviewed by at least three people prior to sending it to apply for a job.

This review should catch spelling and grammatical errors and give you a chance to react to questions from the reviewer (e.g., "Is this statement really needed?" "What does this statement really say?").

PHYSICAL ATTRIBUTES OF A RESUME
* NOTES *

CHAPTER 19
HOW TO PREPARE AN E-RESUME

E-mailing your resume is easy if you understand how e-mail and the Internet work. The best way to post your resume online is to copy and paste it from your word processing program into the e-form. On most sites, there is a field called "Body of Resume" or "Resume" where you can paste your e-resume. For the best results, you need to transform the hardcopy version of your resume before you copy and paste it into the web site's resume form.

How About an Attachment?

Many Internet users think they should send their resumes as attachments to their e-mail messages. They assume that formatted documents that are attached will arrive as sent and be easily opened at the other end. This isn't always the case. Here are four reasons why you should not send your resume as an attachment to an e-mail message.

1. Employers may choose not to open attachments, as they are known to carry viruses.

2. Your Internet Service Provider may not be compatible with the employer's Provider, making your attachment impossible to open on the receiving end.

3. You and the potential employer may be on different computer platforms (e.g., Macintosh, Windows, or UNIX), making the attachments unable to be received.

4. You and the potential employer may have different word-processing software programs or versions that make attachments impossible to open; or if opened, they may be unreadable.

 Don't count on the employer going to any extra effort to convert your attachment. Chances are, your e-mail and attachment will be entirely deleted.

If a job posting specifically asks that your resume be sent as an attachment, follow the instructions provided and assume the employer is capable of opening and reading it. This is basically a question of "Can You Follow Instructions?"

HOW TO PREPARE AN E-RESUME

Save as Text Only, Plain Text, or Notepad

A Text Only, Plain Text, or Notepad document works best for posting your resume online. If you want to have your resume e-mail-ready, you can save work by converting your document to Text Only or Plain Text.

Here's how to convert to Text Only and Plain Text:
a. Open the MS Word document that contains your resume.
b. Click File in your toolbar and select Save As.
c. Type in a new name for this document in File Name, such as "ResTextOnly."
d. Under this is a Save As Type pull-down menu. From this list, select "Text Only (*.txt)." If you're on a Windows XP computer, select "Plain Text" from the pull-down menu.
e. Click Save to perform the conversion.
f. Now close the document but stay in MS Word.
g. Reopen the document you just closed by going to File in the toolbar, click Open, select the file named "ResTextOnly.txt," and click Open. Warning: If you exit MS Word and then open the resume document by clicking on its icon in the directory, it will become a Notepad document-not what you want if you intend to use this version to prepare an e-mailable resume.

Here's how to convert to Notepad:
a. Open the MS Word document that contains your resume.
b. Click File in your toolbar and select Save As.
c. Type in a new name for this document in File Name, such as "ResNotepad."
d. Under this is the Save As Type pull-down menu. From this list, select "TextOnly (*txt)."
e. Click Save to perform the conversion.
f. Now close the document and reopen it by clicking on its icon in the directory.

It will automatically open as a Notepad document (named "ResNotepad.txt"). After converting your resume to either Text Only, Plain Text, or Notepad, what appears in your document window is your resume stripped of any fancy formatting. You are now ready to make a few final adjustments before posting it online.

Delete references to page two

If your resume is more than one page, delete any indications of page breaks such as "Page 1 of 2," "Continued," and your name or header on page 2. Technically, you are making your resume appear as one continuous electronic document.

Use all CAPS for words that need special emphasis

Since Text Only, Plain Text, or Notepad stripped your resume of all boldface, underlines, and italics used for highlighting works, use all capitalized letters to draw attention to important words, phrases, and headings. For the best overall effect, use all caps sparingly and judiciously.

HOW TO PREPARE AN E-RESUME

Replace each bullet point with a standard keyboard symbol

Special symbols such as bullet points, arrows, triangles, and check marks do not transfer well electronically. Therefore, you must change each to a standard keyboard symbol. Suggested replacements are:
- Plus signs (+)
- Dashes (-)
- Asterisks (*)
- Double asterisks (**)

Use the space bar to place a single space immediately after each symbol (and before the words). Do not use the Tab key for spacing as you may have done in your original resume. Also, allow the lines to wrap naturally at the end of a line – don't put a forced return (don't push the Return or Enter key) if it's not the end of the statement, and don't indent the second line of a statement with either the Tab key or Space bar).

Use straight quotes in place of curly quotes

Like bullet points and other special symbols, curly (smart) quotes do not transfer accurately (in fact, they may appear as little rectangles on the recipient's screen). Therefore, replace curly quotes with straight quotes.

To do this, select the text that includes the quotes you want to change. Click Format in your toolbar and select AutoFormat. Click the Options button, and make sure Replace Straight Quotes with Smart Quotes is not selected under both the AutoFormat and AutoFormat As You Type tabs. Then click OK to exit the AutoFormat box, and your curly quotes will be changed to straight quotes.

Rearrange text if necessary

Do a line-by-line review of your document to make sure there are no odd-looking line wraps, extra spaces, or words scrunched together in the body. Make adjustments accordingly. This may require inserting commas between items that were once in columns and are now in paragraph format because tabs and tables disappeared when the document was converted to Text Only or Notepad.

Limit line lengths

Because each type of e-mail software limits the number of characters and spaces per line, your e-mail may have a longer line length than the receiver of your e-mail. This can cause the employer to see line wraps in unusual places, making your resume document look odd and even illogical.

To avoid this problem, limit each line to no more than 65 characters (including spaces), since this is a conservative line length. Here's an easy way to make line length changes in your document:
a. Select the entire document and change the font to Courier, 12 pt.
b. Click File on your toolbar; select Page Setup (Windows XP users will find Page Setup under File in their toolbars); set the left margin at 1 inch and your right margin at 1.75 inch. (Yahoo E-mail users set your right margin at 2.5.)
c. Select the entire document and change the font to Times, Arial, or some other standard font you like.

With the side margins set under these conditions, each line of your document will be no more than 65 characters and spaces.

HOW TO PREPARE AN E-RESUME

A test run

Even if you've followed all these instructions to the letter, it's a good idea to do a few quick test runs. Start by simply e-mailing your message back to yourself to see how it comes in. If it looks OK, then test it further by sending it to a friend on a different Internet Service Provider to check that nothing in your document changes when e-mailed. If all goes well, you can be reasonably confident that when you e-mail your resume to an employer, he or she will receive exactly what you have carefully prepared.

TAKE ACTION

After following the preceding conversion and cleanup procedures, you should have an e-mail-ready resume that you can use over and over again for e-mailing and posting to e-forms.

Your format will not change, but you will still need to tailor your wording to each job you are applying for.

If you have posted your obituary resume on e-forms and company web sites, you should go back and revise or substitute your targeted advertisement resume for the original you have posted.

Your results will be quite different. See the following two examples of a resume, one standard and the other in an e-resume text format.

Standard Resume

RUTH BRAWLEY
212 Blue Smoke Road, Garner, NC 27580   (919) 656-xxxx   rbrawley@hotmail.com

OBJECTIVE
Administrative Assistant with Automated CPA's bringing 15+ years of experience and recent certification plus highly developed skills in computers (70 wpm), listening, time management, customer service, and problem solving.

CERTIFICATION
Administrative Assistant, Wake Tech Community College, Raleigh, NC   2005

RELATED EXPERIENCE
Receptionist, Jones, Smith & Miller CPA's, Raleigh, NC   7 years
- **Provided front office interface with clients and handled most problems without referral to partners.**
- **Set priorities for assigned work each morning and delegated some tasks to clerk and performed other tasks as time permitted, but always completed needed work on the required day.**
- Met an average of 30 clients a day, some scheduled and some walk-ins, and courteously greeted and lined up personnel that answered their questions.

Customer Service Representative, AFLAC, Raleigh, NC   5 years
- Typed (70 wpm) letters and reports from drafts prepared by managers and consistently met deadlines.
- Ordered supplies, met with sales persons, checked inventory, filed, and performed all required duties that resulted in an efficient operation.

Secretary, White Trucking Company, Gastonia, NC   3+ years
- Answered 16-line phone system with courtesy, handled 50% of questions personally, and never left a customer on hold for more than 30 seconds.
- Prepared 60% of correspondence replies without bothering staff members.
- Scheduled location of trucks each morning that provided managers with the ability to pick up additional payloads.

OTHER EXPERIENCE
Stay-at-home Mom, Raleigh, NC   4 years
- **Learned life skills in listening, budgeting, and organizing that are ever present at work.**

COMPUTER SKILLS
Keyboarding speed (70 wpm)
Advanced in all Microsoft programs
Intermediate in Quicken

EDUCATION
General Education Courses, Cape Fear Community College, Wilmington, NC

ACTIVITIES
Competitive softball
Neighborhood watch volunteer

HOW TO PREPARE AN E-RESUME

E-Resume Text Format

RUTH BRAWLEY
212 Blue Smoke Road, Garner, NC 27580 (919)656-1235 rbrawley@hotmail.com

OBJECTIVE
Administrative Assistant with Automated CPA's bringing 15+ years of experience and recent certification plus highly developed skills in computers (70 wpm), listening, time management, customer service, and problem solving.

CERTIFICATION
Administrative Assistant, Wake Tech Community College, Raleigh, NC   2005

RELATED EXPERIENCE
Receptionist, Jones, Smith & Miller CPA's, Raleigh, NC   7 years
* Provided front office interface with clients and handled most problems without referral to partners.
* Set priorities for assigned work each morning and delegated some tasks To clerk and performed other tasks as time permitted, but always completed needed work on the required day.
* Met an average of 30 clients a day, some scheduled and some walk-ins, and courteously greeted and lined up personnel that answered their questions.

Customer Service Representative, AFLAC, Raleigh, NC   5 years
* Typed (70 wpm) letters and reports from drafts prepared by managers and consistently met deadlines.
* Ordered supplies, met with sales persons, checked inventory, filed, and performed all required duties that resulted in an efficient operation.

Secretary, White Trucking Company, Gastonia, NC   3+ years
* Answered 16-line phone system with courtesy, handled 50% of questions personally, and never left a customer on hold for more than 30 seconds.
* Prepared 60% of correspondence replies without bothering staff members.
* Scheduled location of trucks each morning that provided managers with the ability to pick up additional payloads.

OTHER EXPERIENCE
Stay-at-home Mom, Raleigh, NC   4 years
* Learned life skills in listening, budgeting, and organizing that are ever present at work.

COMPUTER SKILLS
Keyboarding speed (70 wpm)
Advanced in all Microsoft programs
Intermediate in Quicken

EDUCATION
GED courses, Cape Fear Community College, Wilmington, NC

ACTIVITIES
Competitive softball
Neighborhood watch volunteer

CHAPTER 20
ARE YOU REALLY EMPLOYABLE?

Have you ever thought about your employability?

Are you physically able to perform the job you are seeking?

How good are your oral communication skills?

These are questions you must answer before you get a job. Everyone's answers will be different, but those answers will determine what you must do to get the job you want.

I have asked students of all ages in my classes about their employability. I get many answers and also many questions. Many students say they think they are discriminated against because of their age, gender, nationality, accent, and appearance. I would like to share my thoughts on the last two items as they are something you can do about them.

Even though applicants may follow the guidelines in this book and have a good resume that fully advertises their skills, many students believe they are turned down for a job before they say the first word in an interview. Your resume has already done its job if you get to the interview. Some of the reasons given for discrimination cannot be changed, but you can certainly do something about your physical appearance and your communication skills. What happens when you are really overweight and you mumble or talk too fast?

Will a potential employer look past the weight and communication issues and give you an opportunity to show your experience and skills? Is it too late to change that initial impression that you might be an insurance risk or stereotyped to be lazy or can't talk well with other employees or customers? Either way, this is something you need to think about and something you can change. Many students have come to me after class to discuss these two exact issues because they are getting interviews but no offers. The fact that the subject comes up and is recognized as possible problems in getting a job offer makes me tell students that the situation is only in their hands and they need to change to be competitive for a job. You can work at changing your appearance, compensate for an accent by speaking clearly and at a moderate speed, or take a class to improve your English or elocution skills.

Your appearance is part of the chemistry of who you are and the impression you make on others. You must realize that chemistry is the main reason for the interview to see if you fit in to the culture of the organization where you are being interviewed. You must be neat, clean, polite, and able to communicate well. But you also need to think about the attributes you have to offer. If you are too heavy or don't speak well, you need to "bite the bullet" and make a decision that will affect you the rest of your life.

Is your personal life in order?

I have experienced many students who were looking for work but couldn't because of their personal situations. I am talking about individuals going through divorce and have never worked

ARE YOU REALLY EMPLOYABLE?

before, child care issues, child custody issues, can't work until child goes to school, and have to be home before the child gets out of school.

These items sound simple but are very complicated when it becomes personal. Even if the individual has time to work, their mind and thoughts are not on the work that must be done. Your priorities are in the right order - taking care of family and self but will that pay your bills.

Please look at your personal self and do the proper soul searching until you decide that you can get a job and give it the proper attention to succeed. Until you do this, you are really no good to yourself, your family, or your employer. The pay for daydreaming, constant worrying and making personal calls on the job is not very good.

You will have to make some tough decisions, but you must get your act together before you become a real candidate for a job.

Thoughts on other employability questions

Q. What would a potential employer think of a male who had facial hair (mustache, goatee, or beard)?

A. I recommend that you not let this be a factor. Go to the interview clean-shaven and then you don't have to worry. Once hired, you can see what the real culture of your new employer is and then adjust to how best to fit into the organization.

Q. Do you look in good physical condition or are you overweight?

A. This is a hard question to answer. Overweight people may be an insurance risk or give the impression of being lazy, and both will hurt you in comparison to your competitors for a job. Don't take the chance. Check with your doctor, go on a diet or some kind of weight-loss program, and feel good about yourself and your chances to get a job.

Q. What is your telephone voice like?

A. You need to be relaxed and speak with confidence over the phone as that may be the first and only contact you have with a potential employer. Pretend you are talking directly to them and maintain good eye contact and focus even though you are on the phone. Do not be nervous and walk while you talk. Keep water available in case the conversation is longer than expected.

Q. Do I really want to go back to work after an early retirement or a regular retirement?

A. The fact that the question even comes up probably means that you are mentally not ready to go back to work. Many factors will impact your final decision - health, proximity of potential work, location of children and grandchildren, financial status, and what you would do if you didn't have a job. Many retirees (and I've had some in classes) have no hobbies and are very restless if they aren't working. Regardless of your situation, once you decide to go back to work, please use the guidelines in this book and prepare a targeted resume tailored to fit the job you want.

 Remember, a hiring manager can determine quickly if you want to work!

CHAPTER 21
FREQUENTLY ASKED QUESTIONS

Q. Is it really necessary to customize each resume before sending it?

A. Yes, you must tailor your resume to every job you apply for. A general resume will probably not get read as it will not include industry-specific wording and offer skills that catch the reviewer's eye to want to read on or to interview you. **(See chapter 16.)**

Q. Do I need to be visually different with font type and size and color of paper?

A. No, use white or off-white paper and print in black using an easy-to-read font type. It is not the font or paper that gets you the interview; it's what you have to say about your skills and abilities.

Q. How long should my resume be?

A. Your advertisement resume should be 1 page long. That is plenty of space to properly describe your experience and how good you are. This requires you to be selective and write the most important things you have to offer a potential employer. It also keeps you from rambling and adding statements that don't fit the job when you need to tailor your experience to the job you are seeking. Long-term executives may need 2 pages and technical applicants may also need 2 pages, counting the technical addendum as page 2.

Q. Should I make my resume longer than 1 page if I survived the initial screening and am called for an interview?

A. Yes, it might help the potential employer know more about you, especially if you have done jobs that are closely related to the job that you are interviewing for. That way you could be more valuable to the potential employer than initially thought. It will not help to have a resume longer than one page if it is an obituary resume. The resume, regardless of length, must show the results of each of your tasks.

Q. Should I "blast or shotgun" my resume to potential employers?

A. No, it is better to apply for specific jobs where you can tailor your Objective and work statements to the skills needed for that specific job. If you are "fishing" for a job, it is very difficult to tailor your resume and get the attention needed to interest a potential employer. College graduates are the most frequent users of the "shotgun" approach for resumes, and it may work for some, but the best approach is still the tailored resume targeted to specific jobs.

Q. Should I include a cover letter with all resume submissions?

A. Yes, a cover letter is a personal and different advertisement of how your skills compare to the skills required for the specific job. It is written in first person and could include personal characteristics that might help with the job, but don't go on the resume (work ethics, dependability, multi-task person, and team player/independent). Salary requirements and salary history information, if requested, go on a cover letter and not on the resume.

FREQUENTLY ASKED QUESTIONS

Q. How do I write an effective resume if I'm changing careers?

A. **You** will need to flavor your different work experiences to the new type of job or industry. This is not easy, but must be done to show you have the necessary skills to do the job. (See Chapter 14 on pages 67-76 for a discussion of these topics with examples.)

Q. Should I set up my own web page to showcase my talents?

A. **That** is strictly up to you and should only be done after you have written a resume that talks for you. If the job is a web design job, it would be a good idea to create a web page and showcase your skills. Otherwise, why have a web page if the resume and cover letter you write aren't good enough to get read and create the interest to go to a web page?

Q. All of your examples are basically 1-page advertisement resumes; what do I do with the longer version of my resume that I've been using?

A. **Do** your 1-page advertisement resume first and be sure it is targeted and shows "how good you are." Your longer resume, if properly written, should be taken to the interview and offered to the interviewer at the appropriate time. The longer resume might include more detail and some related jobs that you could do for the company. You must be sure that the longer resume also talks for you. A longer obituary resume will not help you.

Q. What other services do you offer?

A. **Besides** teaching and counseling on resumes, I spend a lot of time writing and re-writing resumes for students and clients. My website www.makeyourresumetalk.com includes tips and information about resumes and how to get individual help on your resume. Please visit this website for more information on available help that follows all the guidelines in this book.

HART'S 25 REMINDERS CHECKLIST

- [ ] Did you bold your name and use all caps in the Heading?
- [ ] Did you use 6 lines in your Heading when 2 lines would do what you want?
- [ ] Is your Heading format pleasing to the eye?
- [ ] Did you write a targeted Objective with a targeted job, targeted company, and the experience and skills you can bring to the targeted job?
- [ ] Is your Objective an offering one rather than an historical or seeking Objective?
- [ ] Is your Objective 3 lines or less?
- [ ] Did you evaluate the skills needed for the targeted job and tailor your resume to support these jobs?
- [ ] Do your Work Experience statements indicate how good you were, quantify measurements of successes, and your impact within the organization?
- [ ] Did you use an action verb to lead each bulleted statement?
- [ ] Did you include just the last 12-15 years of your work experience?
- [ ] Did you combine job titles for the same company and not repeat duties?
- [ ] If you worked for more than 15 years, have you disguised the time factor?
- [ ] Did you support your Objective in your bulleted statements?
- [ ] Did you show your level of ability for your Computer Skills?
- [ ] Did you list your education in the appropriate area of the resume?
- [ ] If you had Military Service, did you include it on your resume?
- [ ] Did you list activities that indicate your chemistry and will not subject you to discrimination?
- [ ] Did you use 12-pt font (11-pt font as a minimum) for the resume?
- [ ] If you speak more than one language, have you mentioned this fact?
- [ ] Have you prepared a list of references, but have not included them or made reference to them on the resume?
- [ ] Did you bold your entire targeted Objective, 2 or 3 complete statements that best support your Objective, your related job titles, and your related degree and major?
- [ ] Have you proofread your resume in hard copy and corrected any mistakes?
- [ ] Did you get 3 people to read your resume before you sent it to a potential employer?
- [ ] Did you check to see if the information above your thumb line was enticing to potential employers?
- [ ] Did you look at the format to be sure it was easy to read and attractive?

APPENDIX – A
RESUME A BEFORE REVISIONS
CRYSTAL S. WOOD

2054 Vincent Drive
Apex, NC 28672

Home: (919) 612-xxxx
Cell: (919) 376-xxxx

SUMMARY
- AR Management with experience in Credit, Collections, Cash Application, AR Close/Reporting and General Ledger Reconciliation
- Hands-on experience using Microsoft Office, AS 400, Great Plains, JD Edwards, Syteline, Softpak and SAP software

PROFESSIONAL EXPERIENCE

Accounts Receivable Supervisor: (2004 to 2005)
ABC Industries. Raleigh, NC
Management of ten AR departmental employees with cash application, collection and mailroom responsibilities. Responsibilities included AR/GL reconciliation, corporate reports, monitoring branch write-off compliance, journal entry preparation and review, researching bank discrepancies, processing of multiple cash application functions and transactions, enforcing policies and procedures for departmental and branch locations, and assisting internal and external auditors.

Accomplishments Include:
- Preparing the AR Department for Sarbanes-Oxley Compliance.
- Reconstructing the procedure by which thousands of refunds were processed by transitioning to a Global process devoid of the endless keystrokes, approvals and errors that have occurred in the past. This will bring the organization back into compliance with the Fair Credit Practices Act and the Escheat Regulations.
- Rewriting the AR Departmental Procedure Manual and creating a Manager Trainee Manual for Branch Locations

Strengths:
- **Team Leadership. My most significant asset is the ability to gather people together and focus their efforts in a direction that will benefit each individual, the department and accomplish the company's goals.**
- Experience: Full Circle Accounts Receivable Experience within different industries over a 15 year period.
- Strong Work Ethic and Integrity

AR ANALYST: (2002 to March 2004)
RFK Corp., Cary, NC. Accounting Service Center.
Full circle AR functions for various manufacturing sites. Duties include cash application, management of inter-company receivables, collections, invoicing, financial reporting, AR close and GL reconciliation for SAP and Syteline Accounting Systems.

Accomplishments Include:
- **Year end closing at 4% past due over 1 day accompanied by a December record collections that exceeded RFK's highest expectations by 4.5 million.**
- Established the reporting necessary to support RFK goals, set forth the actions and teamwork necessary to accomplish them and ended 2003 at 100% auditable record levels of success.

AR SPECIALIST: (2001 to 2002)
WVIT Pharmaceuticals, Morrisville, NC. Marketer of pharmaceuticals.
Accounts Receivable Management. Activities included cash applications, bank deposits, collections and the research of disputed items. Deduction activity and research was intensive. Performed monthly AR close and GL reconciliation. Corporate reports include DSO, past percentage analysis, collection status, cash flow and audit reports.

Accomplishments Include:
- Managing Cash Transactions for an AR volume of over 500 million/year

FINANCIAL TOOL SPECIALIST: (1998 to 2001)
Carbide Crop Science, RTP NC. Manufacturer and marketer of crop protection chemicals.
Worked within the Carbide Integration Team where I was responsible for the input, maintenance, compliance and tracking of merger synergies. Worked proactively to support Senior Management in US headquarters and parent company in Paris by tracking and documenting merger synergies and costs. Reporting relationship was to the VP Supply Chain & IT.

Accomplishments Include:
- Management of ERI Software and finalization of the Merger Related Synergy Projects
- Refined Written and Oral Skills by working with teams at all levels within the organization and International Parent
- Provided documentation instrumental to Senior Management for budget development under the reorganized structure.

Also worked within the Supply Chain as a Customer Account Coordinator, where I was responsible for supply chain activities such as receiving and processing customer orders, the logistical placement of product to meet demand, invoicing, dispute resolution, sales program administration, suggestive selling and sales support. Took a proactive role in informing the sales force and customers of product and inventory issues and provided recommendations on product movement.

APPENDIX – A

Duties include shipment tracing, return processing, system report preparation, spreadsheet generation and analysis. Also served as a team safety steward, where I have coordinated and conducted safety lectures.

BILLING & REVENUE COORDINATOR: (1996 to 1998)
City of Hickory, Hickory, NC. Local municipality with a receivable customer base of approximately 18000 customers. Responsible for the receivable accounts of the City of Hickory. Receivable billings included water and sewer accounts, garbage, public services, grants, cemeteries, renters, tuition reimbursement, parking, donations, sewer surcharge, building inspections and all other miscellaneous contractual accounts. Worked actively with the accounting division on general ledger account reconciliation. Duties included the processing and approval of all adjustments and refunds, bad check reversals, Shuford Garden refunds, collections, receivable analysis, bad debt preparation, rate changes, billing system changes and the management of two departmental employees.
Accomplishments Include:
- Effective Contract Review and Contract Compliance
- Improvement of AR Receivable Base for all Miscellaneous Billings
- Improvements regarding GL/AR Reconciliation and New Account Setup
- Improved Customer Service Skills by working with residential and commercial customers accompanied with my interaction with various levels of Management within the City.

CORPORATE CREDIT MANAGER: (1993 to 1996)
Brooks Brothers, Inc., Hickory, NC. Manufacturer of hosiery, health products and men's apparel.
Responsible for the operations and efficiency of the Credit and Collections department. Worked effectively with senior management in the accomplishment of the company's goals by establishing departmental policies and procedures. Responsibilities included budgeting, benchmarking, contract review and renewals, letters of international credit and management of four departmental employees for four divisional product lines.

Accomplishments included

- Reducing the Past due Percentages and DSO by 50%.
- Reduced Bad Debts by Developing Credit Files and Credit Checks
- Incorporated company acquisitions within the credit and accounts receivable departments.
- Served on Creditor's Committee

DIVISIONAL CREDIT MANAGER: (1988 TO 1993)
Brooks Brothers, Inc., Wilkesboro, NC. Hosiery/Apparel Manufacturer.
Credit management of accounts among four different divisions at a total estimated volume of one hundred million per year. Responsibilities included financial analysis of new and existing accounts, setting credit lines, advising factor protection, and the collection of all past due invoices and disputed accounts.
Accomplishments Include:
- Successfully incorporated our wholesale division from a previously factored position to in-house credit approvals.
- Maintained an AR Past Due Balance of less than 5% over 30 days.
- Participated in Customer Visits and Improved Overall Customer Relations.

EDUCATION
Bachelor of Science in Business Administration. May 1983. Appalachian State University, Boone, NC. Business program with double major in marketing and economics.
- Coastal Carolina Community College, Jacksonville, NC. Classes: COBOL, Programming Concepts I and II.
- Catawba County Community College, Hickory, NC. Two refresher Accounting Courses.
- AMA Advanced Financial Analysis, Excel classes and various Dun & Bradstreet courses.

APPENDIX – A
Richard's Critique of Resume A

- ✓ The resume uses Summary rather than Objective, and the Summary is historical and does not show what the applicant has to offer or the job the applicant wants.

- ✓ The computer skills are listed in the Summary but are not supported, nor does it show the level of ability for any of them.

- ✓ The Experience section is written in paragraph format rather than individual bulleted statements. The paragraph format tends to blend information and the most important item may be last and never read.

- ✓ The Experience section includes comments about the companies. This is the applicant's resume, not the company's. If the information is important to tell your story, work the information into one of the bulleted statements.

- ✓ The "Responsible for" and "duties included" statements do not really say what the applicant did. This usually comes from copying statements from job descriptions and is what the applicant was supposed to do. Someone else may have done the work and the resume needs to say what the applicant actually did and how good she was.

- ✓ The accomplishments are mostly just tasks, not real accomplishments. Listing them separately does not show what the applicant did, and therefore, it is hard to show the effort to achieve any accomplishment.

- ✓ Part of the resume is written in first person. Resumes should be written in third person so the "I's and My's" need to be changed.

- ✓ Job information goes on one line and should state job title (bold), company name, location, and dates.

- ✓ The resume includes no outside activities to show the applicant's chemistry.

- ✓ The font size is too small. It should be 12-pt size.

Resume A After Revisions

CRYSTAL S. WOOD
2054 Vincent Drive, Apex, NC 28672   (H) (919) 612-xxxx   (C) (919) 376-xxxx

OBJECTIVE
Accounts Receivable Manager with Red Hat bringing 15 years of experience and skills in accounts receivable analysis, insight, integrity, team leadership and customer relations that create business partnerships, inspire process improvements and minimize losses.

RELATED EXPERIENCE
Accounts Receivable Manager, ABC Industries, Raleigh, NC   2004 - 2005
- Managed 10 employees with 5 direct reports and redesigned the refund process to a global download procedure that saved $160,000 the first year plus annual savings of $70,000.
- Refined the AR Procedural manuals and procedural flowcharts and trained employees on policies that ensured Sarbanes-Oxley Compliance.
- Conducted and reviewed multiple cash application processes and journal entries that prevented reconciliation issues and ensured proper revenue reporting.

Accounts Receivable Specialist, RFK Corp, Cary, NC   2002 – 2004
- Achieved 96% current collections results and exceeded collection goal by $4.5 million.

Accounts Receivable Specialist, WVIT Pharmaceuticals, Morrisville, NC   2001 – 2002
- Transacted all cash applications, collections, deduction review, and manual deposits for a sales volume of over 500 million without assistance.

Financial Tool Specialist, Carbide Crop Science, RTP, NC   1998 – 2001
- Brought together teams of individuals by exhibiting team leadership, negotiation skills and analytical abilities that ensured compliance with synergy objectives and accurately reported those achievements to parent company in Paris.
- Minimized bad debt by analyzing high-risk accounts and provided exceptional customer service through building working relationships based on respect and integrity.

Billing and Revenue Coordinator, City of Hickory, Hickory, NC   1996–1998
- Reviewed, monitored and managed the compliance of all new and existing billing contracts that ensured accurate revenue generation.
- Ensured compliance with the general ledger and supplied exceptional customer service by avoiding reconciliation issues and provided support in researching discrepancies.

Corporate/Divisional Credit Manager, Brooks Brothers, various NC locations 1988-1996
- Restructured collection activities and credit training of a staff of 10 in separate divisions that set the tone for making credit decisions and avoided $40,000 in bad debt for a single account.
- Forecasted bad debts, prepared budgets, negotiated contracts, selected external collection agencies, and created AR structure that reduced AR balance by 30% in first year.

EDUCATION
BS Business Administration, Appalachian State University, Boone, NC.

ACTIVITIES
Toastmasters   SWOOP   Former member of USA Triathlon   Caregivers Association

APPENDIX – A

Resume B Before Revisions

RUTH BRAWLEY

212 Blue Smoke Road, Garner, NC 27580   (919) 656-xxxx   rbrawley@hotmail.com

Introduction   Administrative Assistant

Work Experience

    1998-2005 Jones, Smith & Miller CPA's, Raleigh, NC
    Receptionist
    Worked in the front office and scheduled appointments
    Set priorities and delegated some tasks to the clerk

    1992-1997 AFLAC Insurance, Raleigh, NC
    Customer Service Rep
    Handled all phone calls
    Typed letters and reports
    Ordered supplies and assisted Sales personnel

    1987-1992 Unemployed, Stay-at-home Mom

    1983-1987 White Trucking Company, Gastonia, NC

    Answered phones and handled questions
    Answered letters and scheduled truck locations

Education

    GED courses, Cape Fear Community College, Wilmington, NC

Computer Skills

    Microsoft Office, Quicken, and Outlook

Training

    2005 Administrative Assistant Training, Wake Technical CC, Raleigh, NC

References available upon request

APPENDIX – A
Richard's Critique of Resume B

- ✓ The resume uses Introduction rather than Objective, and the Introduction does not show what the applicant has to offer. The applicant should use a targeted Objective.

- ✓ The training shown under the Professional Development section was actually a Certification program and should go right under the Objective.

- ✓ The information under the side headings should be indented under the headings rather than perpendicular after the longest heading.

- ✓ Job information goes on one line and should state job title (bold), company name, location, and dates.

- ✓ Dates go on the far right since what you have done is more important than when it was done.

- ✓ All of the work statements are just tasks with no indication how well the applicant performed these tasks.

- ✓ The computer skills are listed, but the section does not show the level of ability for any of them.

- ✓ The resume includes no outside activities to show the applicant's chemistry.

RESUME (B) AFTER REVISIONS

RUTH BRAWLEY
212 Blue Smoke Road, Garner, NC 27580   (919) 656-xxxx   rbrawley@hotmail.com

OBJECTIVE
Administrative Assistant with Automated CPA's bringing 15+ years of experience and recent certification plus highly developed skills in computers (70 wpm), listening, time management, customer service, and problem solving.

CERTIFICATION
Administrative Assistant, Wake Tech Community College, Raleigh, NC   2005

RELATED EXPERIENCE
Receptionist, Jones, Smith & Miller CPA's, Raleigh, NC   7 years
- **Provided front office interface with clients and handled most problems without referral to partners.**

- **Set priorities for assigned work each morning and delegated some tasks to clerk and performed other tasks as time permitted, but always completed needed work on the required day.**
- Met an average of 30 clients a day, some scheduled and some walk-ins, and courteously greeted and lined up personnel that answered their questions.

Customer Service Representative, AFLAC, Raleigh, NC   5 years
- Typed (70 wpm) letters and reports from drafts prepared by managers and consistently met deadlines.
- Ordered supplies, met with sales persons, checked inventory, filed, and performed all required duties that resulted in an efficient operation.

Secretary, White Trucking Company, Gastonia, NC   3+ years
- Answered 16-line phone system with courtesy, handled 50% of questions personally, and never left a customer on hold for more than 30 seconds.
- Prepared 60% of correspondence replies without bothering staff members.
- Scheduled location of trucks each morning that provided managers with the ability to pick up additional payloads.

OTHER EXPERIENCE
Stay-at-home Mom, Raleigh, NC   4 years
- **Learned life skills in listening, budgeting, and organizing that are ever present at work.**

COMPUTER SKILLS
Keyboarding speed (70 wpm)
Advanced in all Microsoft programs
Intermediate in Quicken

EDUCATION
General Education Courses, Cape Fear Community College, Wilmington, NC

ACTIVITIES
Competitive softball
Neighborhood watch volunteer

APPENDIX – A

Resume C Before Revisions

BEVERLY DONNELLY
105 Gravel Lane
Chapel Hill, NC 27514

Home: (919) 984-xxxx
Cell: (919) 602-xxxx

bdonnelly@hotmail.com

Career Profile
Accounting Professional with over 20 years' experience in retail, wholesale, distribution and manufacturing in small to large corporate structure. Working and educational background with Generally Accepted Accounting Principles, Standard Audit Practices and Sarbanes Oxley Act. Proven ability in Treasury, Finance, Budget, Internal Controls, Taxes, Capital Expenditures Audit, Organizational Development, Licensing and Contract Negotiations. Excellent written and verbal communication provides efficient and favorable interaction with all levels of staff, management, customers and associates. Exceptional ability to lead staff in performing multitasks efficiently, accurately and within stringent deadlines. Ability to handle/lead special projects while performing current work assignments. Team player, astute planner and negotiator. Proactive in recognizing problems and implementing solutions; highly analytical.

Industry Knowledge
♦   Comprehensive knowledge of the practices and operations of

- Health and Beauty,
- Warehousing
- Retail and Wholesale Fuel
- Beverage Industry
- Construction
- Upscale Time Pieces
- Hospitality Industry,
- Convenience Stores,

Technology Application
♦   PC, Mainframe and Internet proficient.
♦   Demonstrated use of advanced computer skills to identify and solve problems.
♦   Proven working ability with industry specific software as well as MS Office, including Excel, Word, Power Point, Access, Monarch, FTP, PDF and Adobe. Ability to excel with integrated accounting, finance, HR/Payroll and data mining software.

Professional Experience:

2000-2005 Custer's Handy Stores LLC, Chapel Hill, NC
Vice President of Finance and IT   2001–2005   **Controller/Assistant Controller**   2000–2001

Senior Financial Executive with leadership and decision-making responsibility for the development of this 200+ million corporation's finance functions. Challenged to rebuild and revitalize corporate accounting, financial systems and budgeting, restore financial credibility within and outside the organization during and after Chapter 11 bankruptcy (formerly Handy Stores USA) and subsequent emergence to CUSTERS' LLC. Scope of responsibility expanded to include Information Technology and Human Resources. Focused efforts on developing bank relationships, strengthening corporate business infrastructure, introducing sound consistent financial policies and implementing advanced information technologies. Supervised 24 person corporate office staff.

- Directed development of Access Database and accounting controls resulting in eliminating a $3,500,000 annual receivable write-off.
- Cash flow reporting daily/weekly/monthly with accurate projections for future periods that allowed organization to co-ordinate spending to incoming receipts.
- Organized the efforts of three departments resulting in accurate, timely, monthly financials being published with 40% less staff.
- Managed critical relationships and negotiations, including their financial analysis, ROI and cost effectiveness with auditors, bankers, attorney's, insurance brokers, Cap-ex and IT infra structure upgrades.
- Retained all essential personnel during two year Chapter 11 bankruptcy proceeding.
- Expert negotiation resulting in over a $150,000 reduction in cost of office space while increasing the quality of the work environment over 100%.

APPENDIX – A

1995–2000 Manager of Retail Accounting – Hawaii Oil LTD, Honolulu, HI
Responsible for the financial controls, organization and co-ordination between the operations, marketing, terminal and financial group of the retail division and wholesale fuel.
- Developed in-house process tracking of purchase requests for capital expenditures, allocating repairs & maintenance and truck revenue resulting in a $1M savings.
- Customized software to the needs of executives and operations resulting in over a $550,000 savings in the cost of supplies, and a $950,000 increase in gross margin annually.
- Improved Accounts Payable timing resulting in better cash flow.

1989–1995 Treasurer and Co-Owner - Donnelly & Sons Corp., Honolulu, HI
Co-Owner and operator of $1.5M net profit, cosmetic and fragrance wholesale, warehouse and distribution operation. Conducted business on the islands of Oahu, Maui, Hawaii, Guam and the Philippines. Staff of fifteen people.
- Evaluated, installed and managed integrated software system for Inventory, A/P, A/R, and G/L LIBRA software.
- Initiated inventory controls resulting in less than .02% shrink/spoilage ratio
- Coordinated construction and launch of Guerlain Boutique.

1987–1989 Accounts Receivable Manager - Outrigger Hotels, Honolulu, HI
Largest chain of hotels in the state of Hawaii. Managed a staff of twenty five responsible for billing over $2M revenue per week from 23 properties.
- Realigned department to parallel marketing classification of properties creating improved inter-department relations and employee performance.
- Improved accuracy and timeliness of billing while shortening work week.

1983-1986 Mgr. of Financial Controls, 1985–1986, Mgr. General Accounting, 1983–1985
Carlos of the Ritz Group, LTD, New York, NY
Managed consolidation of all domestic financial activity including consolidation of worldwide activities for parent company; Halo Pharmaceutical. Strong inter-company and inter-department relations.
- Restructured procedure for monthly statement consolidation resulting in shortening preparation by four days.
- Prepared financial/narrative justification for capital appropriations.
- Created Lotus program for profitability of individual brands and monthly flash reports of net profit variances for top management.

1978-1982 Mgr. Financial Planning, 1982–83 (promotion), Assistant Controller U.S. and Territories, 1979–82, Mgr. Domestic Accounting, 1978-79, Canada Dry Corp., NY, NY
Coordinated and prepared for domestic operations consolidated annual profit plan, monthly reporting and cash flow for this multi million dollar company.
- Prepared financial/narrative justification for capital appropriations
- Distinguished performance in conducting internal audit of accounting, tax, marketing department and inventory/fixed assets improving compliance with SEC requirements.

Education
Hawaii Pacific University, Honolulu, HI, MBA, May 1999, elected class representative and President
- Queens College, CUNY, Queens, NY, BA, Accounting Major. January 1980
- Passing grade in three parts of CPA exam, New York, NY 1981

APPENDIX – A

Richard's Critique of Resume C

- ✓ The Objective should be targeted and should include the skills the applicant has to offer to support the targeted job. Many resume writers use a profile, but it is all historical and doesn't say what the applicant wants to do now (next). It reads well but all blends together because of its length.

- ✓ In the Industry knowledge section, there are many misplaced commas. This usually occurs because it was not carefully read after preparation.

- ✓ In the Technology Application, many skills are shown, but the real level of ability is missing. Words like "demonstrated ability," "proven ability," and "ability to excel" are not really definitive and could be misleading.

- ✓ Dates go on the far right since what you have done is more important than when it was done.

- ✓ The paragraphs or statements right under each job line are informative but would be better served if they were combined as bulleted statements with what looks like bulleted accomplishment statements. However, many of these "accomplishment" statements are really just tasks with no results.

- ✓ The numbers used are inconsistent. One place it says $1.5M and another place it shows $3,500,000. Numbers should be shown consistently and are best shown by using $1.5 million, rather than using K and M to mean thousands and millions.

- ✓ "Responsible for" statements do not really say what the applicant did. Someone else may have done the work, and the resume needs to say what the applicant accomplished.

- ✓ The experience shown goes back 26 years when only 12-15 years are needed. The applicant needs to be current as systems and technology change so quickly.

- ✓ Under Education, show the degree and major first and bold both items. Do not show the dates of degrees older than 10 years.

- ✓ Showing that the applicant passed 3 parts of the CPA exam 23 years ago doesn't mean much if there is no interest in completing the exam. The retention period has already expired.

- ✓ The resume includes no outside activities to show the applicant's chemistry.

APPENDIX – A

Resume C After Revisions

BEVERLY DONNELLY
105 Gravel Lane, Chapel Hill, NC 27514   (919) 984-xxxx (h)   (919) 602-xxxx   bdonnelly@hotmail.com

JOB OBJECTIVE:
Controller with QuickStop bringing the experience, knowledge, and passion of 15+ years of progressive accounting and technology and skills in acquisition analysis, documentation, financial controls, modeling, and negotiating contracts.

PROFESSIONAL EXPERIENCE:

Vice President of Finance and IT, Custer's Handy Stores LLC, Chapel Hill, NC   5 years
- Used thorough knowledge of Generally Accepted Accounting Principles (GAAP), Sarbanes Oxley Act, business law and licensing in developing accurate and complete financial statements that were certified by independent auditors with no recommendations for changes.
- **Recognized and resolved a $3½ million annual cash loss after developing and implementing technology advanced internal controls.**

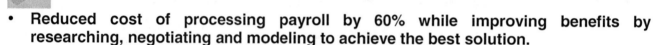

- **Reduced cost of processing payroll by 60% while improving benefits by researching, negotiating and modeling to achieve the best solution.**
- Initiated upgrades to servers and telecommunications equipment that reduced down time to less than 1% and a positive return on investment in one year.
- **Created and presented to the Executive Board financial results and future projections that influenced their direction for the financial success of the company.**
- Played a significant role in regaining or establishing credit terms with vendors that improved cash flow by over $1 million per month.
- **Organized and implemented the accounting transition of former entity, Handy Stores USA with 156 revenue locations in four states, to Custer's in a 24-hour time frame that complied with acquisition terms and achieved 100% accuracy.**

Manager of Retail Accounting, Hawaii Oil LTD, Honolulu, HI,   5 years
- Developed in-house process tracking system for capital expenditures, repairs and maintenance, and truck revenue that resulted in a $1million savings.
- **Customized software to the needs of executives, sales and operations that resulted in over $550,000 in savings in the cost of supplies and a $950,000 increase in annual gross margin.**

Chief Financial Officer, Donnelly & Sons Corp., Honolulu, HI   5 years
- Evaluated, installed and managed integrated software system for Inventory, A/P, A/R, and G/L that saved $250,000 in labor costs and reduced inventory shrinkage to ½ of 1%.

Also worked as Accounts Receivable Manager in HI and Manager of Financial Controls in NY, where compliance with SEC requirements was improved.

EDUCATION
MBA, Hawaii Pacific University, Honolulu, HI, elected class representative and President
BA/Accounting, Queens Collage, CUNY, Queens, NY

PROFESSIONAL STATUS
Registered to sit for CPA exam in January 2005. Passed three parts previously

ACTIVITIES
Girl Scout   Charity volunteer   Competitive tennis player

APPENDIX-A

Beverly Donnelly

Technical Addendum

Program	Experience Level
Excel	Expert
Word	Intermediate
PowerPoint	Expert
Access	Knowledgeable
Outlook	Expert
Windows me, 2000, NT, 2003	Intermediate
Visio 2000	Knowledgeable
Monarch (data mining)	Expert
QuickBooks	Intermediate
Lotus Notes	Knowledgeable
Resource Management Systems, PDI (integrated financial software)	Expert
Libra Accounting System	Expert
ClarisWorks	Intermediate
Corel Draw	Intermediate
PDF, Jpeg, XML	Intermediate
Right Fax, E-Fax	Expert
ATG readers	Intermediate
Cash Registers	Knowledgeable
Price book/Automated Stock Ledgers	Intermediate

Also worked with various Main Frame systems and networking solutions such as Cable/DSL and Satellite Dish.

APPENDIX – A
Resume D Before Revisions

P.O. Box 221 Phone 410-394-xxxx
Street, MD 21111 E-mail gpenny1@msn.com

GERALDINE PENNY

Career Objective
   To obtain a more challenging position that will allow me to use my background and education in Biology.

Professional Experience
May 1999-Present   **American Red Cross**
                               Laboratory Technologist II
- Extracting DNA from whole blood and filter paper using the Geno-M Robot and Qiagen Spin Columns
- Practicing DNA methodology for SSOP including PCR, gel electrophoresis, PicoGreen, dot-blotting and detection methods
- Performing SSOP by new Luminex/LabType technology (flow cytometry)

August 1996-May 1998   **Marshall University**
                               Teaching/Graduate Assistant
- Taught General Biology Lab for non-majors and Introductory Biology for majors
- Assisted professors with weekly duties
- Assisted with preparation and maintenance of Biology labs

June 1994-August 1994   **E.I. DuPont**
June 1995-August 1995   **Summer Assistant**
- Maintained catalog of chemicals for accuracy and compliance
- Tested strength and durability of nylon filaments using an Instron machine
- Assisted with production of nylon filaments on the extruder
- Determined denier of nylon filaments

Education
   August, 1998 Master of Science in Biology, Marshall University, Huntington, WV
   May, 1996 Bachelor of Science in Biology, Fairmont State College, Fairmont, WV

Relevant Studies
   Green Bottom Swamp Project
   Thesis Research: Life history of Caenis amica (a small mayfly)
- Collected water and insect samples from November 1996 to November 1997
- Conducted head and body measurements at Wheeling Jesuit University using Java Computer System
Presented scientific papers at WV Academy of Science and Association of Southeastern Biologists

APPENDIX – A

Richard's Critique of Resume D

- ✓ The name should always be the first thing a reviewer sees, so move the name above the rest of the heading.

- ✓ Delete the solid line clear across the page as it stops computer scans in certain software.

- ✓ The Objective and the rest of the resume are written in third person, not first, so "me" and "my" must come out of the Objective.

- ✓ The Objective should be targeted and should include the skills the applicant has to offer to support the targeted job.

- ✓ Dates go on the far right since what you have done is more important than when it was done. This also applies to the Education section with the dates moved to the far right.

- ✓ Job information goes on one line and should state job title (bold), company name, location, and dates.

- ✓ All of the work statements are just tasks with no idea how well the applicant performed these tasks.

- ✓ The resume includes no outside activities to show the applicant's chemistry.

APPENDIX – A
Resume D After Revisions

GERALDINE PENNY
P.O. Box 221, Street, MD 21111   410-394-xxxx   gpenny1@msn.com

OBJECTIVE
Environmental Technician with Brook Environmental Corp. bringing 5+ years of Laboratory Technologist experience and skills in testing, analysis, research, and report writing plus Masters degree in Biology.

EXPERIENCE
Laboratory Technologist II, American Red Cross, Baltimore, MD   1999-Present
- **Perform DNA testing from whole blood and filter paper using the Geno-M 96 Robot and Qiagen spin columns that result in accurate DNA readings.**
- Practice DNA methodology for SSOP including PCR, gel electrophoresis, PicoGreen, dot-blotting, and detection methods that result in lab expertise transferable to any industry.
- **Perform SSOP by new Luminex/LabType technology (flow cytometry) that normally result in excellent efficiency and quality, a 0% discrepancy rate, and a 90-100% TAT (turnaround Time).**
- Worked closely with other team members in comparing test study results that ensures accurate and timely analysis from research and tests performed.
- Test between 800 and 1000 samples weekly, including 3 loci of A, B, and DRB.
- Reported results almost always ahead of schedule and with very few mistakes, thus saving money on repeats and supplies.

Teaching/Lab Assistant, Marshall University, Huntington, WV   1996-1998
- Taught two 2-hour labs for General Biology and non-Biology majors consisting of 20-30 students twice a week that provided a GO TO person for questions.
- Set up 3 labs three times a week, made up weekly quizzes, and kept records of all graded material from lab that gave the Professor more time to do research.

Summer Lab Assistant, E. I. DuPont, Parkersburg, WV   Summers 1994, 1995
- Maintained Catalog of Chemicals by checking MSDS's for accuracy and compliance.
- Tested strength and durability of 100-500 nylon filaments daily using an Instron machine with test results used in the production of the filaments.

EDUCATION
MS/Biology, Marshall University, Huntington, WV   1998
BS/Biology, Fairmont State College, Fairmont, WV   1996
Masters Research – Researched, tested, and analyzed the Green Bottom Swamp and wrote thesis on the Life History of the small mayfly after collecting water and insect samples for a year.

COMPUTER SKILLS
Intermediate in Word, WordPerfect, and Access
Knowledgeable in Excel and PowerPoint

ACTIVITIES
Golf   Piano   Reading

APPENDIX – A

Resume E Before Revisions

M. GARY SPARKS

513 Brandywine Avenue • Cary, NC, 27519
Phone (919) 460-xxxx • garysparks@nc.rr.com

OBJECTIVE
Seeking an E-Business, Marketing or Product Management Leadership position where more than 20 years of high-tech experience will contribute.

SUMMARY OF QUALIFICATIONS
E-Business, Marketing and Product Management leadership in a high tech environment. Recent strategic and tactical accomplishments include successful leadership of Nortel Networks Enterprise E-Business group; including initiatives in the development of electronic markets, marketing program management, supply chain management, and customer relationship management. Expertise in Marketing, Competitive Intelligence, E-Commerce, Web Development, New Product Introduction, Finance, Operations, Production Engineering and Manufacturing.

RECENT PROFESSIONAL EXPERIENCE

Tutela Information Security
Founder & Vice-President of Marketing: Cary, NC, (July 2003 – Jan 2005)
Tutela Information Security was founded in July 2003 to provide open source security software and intrusion detection services to consumers and small enterprises.
- Developed business and startup plan for Tutela
- Conducted market segmentation and risk analysis plan.
- Developed corporate and solutions marketing strategy and web site collateral.

Nortel Networks, 1983 to December 2002
Director, Enterprise E-Business: Research Triangle Park, NC, (Jan. 2000 – Dec. 2002)
Responsible to develop and implement E-Business solutions for Enterprise global customers. Led a team of 22 direct and 56 indirect staff located throughout Europe and North America, supporting a $2.5B revenue base.
- Developed marketing and product plans for E-Business Solutions portfolio.
- Strategic and operational responsibility for $55M program budget.
- Successfully implemented transactional connectivity between Nortel and marketing partners, corporate accounts, global partners, stocking distributors, and direct resellers.
- Delivered a business case and led the implementation of a corporate wide quotation /configuration and marketing collateral system.
- Successfully negotiated services contracts with Telecentric, IBM and Netformx.
- Developed a strategy to establish a Telco Industry Electronic Marketplace.
- Introduced B2B Solutions in 2002 that resulted in $50 million worth of operational savings and a 30% increase in the percentage of e-orders.

APPENDIX – A

Senior Manager, Marketing, Wireless Networks: Richardson, Texas, (1999 – 2000)
- Responsible for marketing commercialization, pricing and web operations of Wireless Networks products in support of $3.2B wireless business.
- Established new marketing guidelines for product introductions based on Time-To-Market principles.
- Operational responsibility for @Wireless.com web site achieving 500,000 page views/month.
- Successfully introduced 1XRTT and MTX10 wireless products. Team members participated in 5 additional product programs.

Manager, Wireless Networks: **Calgary, Canada, (1990 – 1999)**
- Manager, Change Management. Led implementation of Customer Value Metrics, Business Management Assessment and Change Management.
- Manager, Field Upgrades. Led a team (6-people direct, 100-people indirect) that developed processes and managed $18 million Known Product Defect provision for the application of engineering changes to Wireless product at the customer site.
- Manager, Manufacturing Program. Led startup of Wireless Manufacturing Program Management team (8-people) responsible for the coordination of 350 operations staff to ramp the new CDMA product line (1996 revenue of $400 million) to production status in less than six months.
- Manager, Wireless Design Transfer. Led the startup of Design Transfer team (7–people) responsible for the intellectual property transfer, from Qualcomm to Nortel in support of a $1 billion contract.
- Manager, Engineering. Led staff of 14 engineers, with $3.5M budget in production engineering of circuit board manufacturing process, outsourcing to Mexico, risk mitigation planning, acquisition transfers, ISO 9000 implementation, and presented Self Directed Work Team (SDWT) successes at numerous Association for Manufacturing Excellence Conferences.

Manager, Manufacturing, Switching Systems: Calgary, Alberta, Canada, (1983 – 1990)
- Manager, Circuit Pack Auto Insertion
- Manager, Circuit Pack Test
- Group Leader and Test Technologist

PRIOR PROFESSIONAL EXPERIENCE
Manager, Sales & Service, Baydala Audiocom Ltd., Calgary, Alberta, Canada (1982-1983)
Technologist, Installation and Commissioning, AEL Microtel Ltd., Brockville, Canada (1981-1982)
Vice President, Operations, El-Mur Jewelers Inc., Sarnia, Ontario, Canada (1977 – 1979)

EDUCATION
MBA, Queen's University, Kingston, Ontario, Canada, 1999
BA Certificate, University of Calgary, Canada – 1987
EET Diploma, DeVry University, Toronto, Canada – 1981

Extensive Nortel training includes courses in finance, marketing, customer service, strategic planning, problem-solving, team-building, leadership, management, ISO certification, total quality control, project management, just-in-time manufacturing, oracle financials, advanced intelligent networks, wireless communications, computer/telephony integration, Frame Relay, TCP/IP and internet (1983 to 2002).

ACHIEVEMENTS
- Top Talent Designation, awarded 2000, 2001, 2002
- Consistently Achieved Exceed rating in Performance.
- Product Line Manufacturing Launch Award (1996)
- Gold Award Sprint PCS Contract (1996)
- President's Award of Excellence, People Development (1993)
- President's Award of Excellence, Staff Support (1993)
- Management Leadership Forum (Levels 1 & 2)

APPENDIX – A

Richard's Critique of Resume E

- ✓ Eliminate the solid line clear across the page under heading as it could prevent a computer scan in certain software.

- ✓ The Objective is seeking and should be an Offering Objective.

- ✓ The Objective is directed at three different jobs. Please tailor your resume to individual jobs. This one would require three different resumes.

- ✓ The Summary of Qualifications mentions accomplishments and successful leadership, but the rest of the resume includes only one accomplishment. Such statements make a reviewer wonder about the other statements. Weave the experience and skills into your targeted objective.

- ✓ The resume states "Recent Professional Experience," and this section goes back over 20 years. Recent experience is 12-15 years.

- ✓ Only one line should be used for job title, company, location, and dates.

- ✓ The resume contains separate information about the companies worked for. This is YOUR resume, not the company's. If this information is important to a potential employer, work it into one of your work statements.

- ✓ Be consistent in the use of dates. Use years/years and don't switch between months/years and years/years.

- ✓ "Responsible for" statements are not useful. They only show what you were supposed to do, not what you actually did.

- ✓ Instead of many job titles for the same company, show the top title and include anything you did for that company that supports the experience and skills you have to offer to the potential employer. Add a couple of bulleted statements to show other skills you can offer.

- ✓ The achievements sound nice in their separate section but are meaningless unless you state what you did to get them. It would be much better to tie them into a task to give you a result.

- ✓ The resume includes no outside activities to show the applicant's chemistry.

APPENDIX – A

Resume E After Revisions

M. GARY SPARKS
513 Brandywine Avenue, Cary, NC, 27519   (919) 460-xxxx   garysparks@nc.rr.com

OBJECTIVE
Marketing Manager with XYZ Company bringing 15+ years of high-tech leadership experience and skills in marketing, e-Business, new product introduction and operations.

RECENT PROFESSIONAL EXPERIENCE
Founder & Vice-President Marketing, Tutela Information Security, Cary, NC   2003 - 2005
- **Developed business and startup plan to provide open source security software and intrusion detection services to consumers and small enterprises that resulted in the partnership startup.**
- Conducted market segmentation and risk analysis plan that resulted in plan to focus on small professional offices.
- Developed corporate and solutions marketing strategy and web site collateral that established company's identity and purpose.

Director, E-Business/ Marketing Manager, Nortel Networks, various locations 1993 - 2002
- **Implemented E-Business solutions for Enterprise global customers by leading a team of 22 direct and 56 indirect staff that resulted in $50 million worth of operational savings.**
- Developed marketing and product plans for E-Business solutions portfolio that resulted in their inclusion as deal enhancers in sales quotes.
- **Delivered a business case and led the implementation of a corporate wide enterprise quotation /configuration and marketing collateral system that significantly improved sales force efficiency.**
- Successfully negotiated service contracts with Telecentric, IBM and Netformx that resulted in E Marketplace capability, EDI implementation outsourcing and product configuration simplification.
- Reduced new product introduction cycle by establishing new marketing guidelines for product introductions based on Time-To-Market principles.
- Managed @Wireless.com web site that achieved 500,000 page-views / month.
- Managed a team of 8 people direct and 200+ people indirect that developed processes and project managed $18 million known product defect provisions and resulted in a record deployment of corrective actions to fix safety and performance issues with installed wireless cell sites.
- Led the introduction of the CDMA wireless product line (1996 revenue of $400 million) that resulted in the fastest manufacturing ramp of a new product line, six months from start to volume production.

Also worked as a financial analyst and manufacturing manager for Nortel.

EDUCATION
MBA, Queen's University, Kingston, Ontario, Canada, 1999
BA Certificate, University of Calgary, Canada
EET Diploma, DeVry University, Toronto, Canada

ACTIVITIES
Marathon runner
Charity volunteer

APPENDIX – A
Resume F Before Revisions

Larry Phipps, M.Ed.
2733 Wake Forest Way
Wake Forest, North Carolina 27587
(919) 665-xxxx   nclp2733@nc.rr.com

Objective
IT project management responsibilities utilizing strengths in business and technology analysis, strategic planning, management, analytical problem solving, communications and follow through. Goal is to lead multi-service information technology projects on time and under budget.

Summary of qualifications
17 years of technical experience and over 13 years in the pharmaceutical industry in server management, project management, desktop development, and programming. Proven ability to grasp business needs, evaluate priorities and apply core technology to deliver prudent enterprise solutions. Proven areas of accomplishment in:

- Customer Relationships Management
- End user training/support
- Project Management
- Communications Skills
- Client/Server Technology
- PC/LAN/WAN Administration
- Risk Assessment
- General Programming Skills

COMPUTER SKILLS

Operating System:	MS-DOS, Windows 3.1, 95, 98, NT 3.5, 4.0, Windows 2000, Windows XP, UNIX, Novell Netware 3 & 4, Sun Solaris 2.5, 2.6
Networking:	LAN, WAN, TCP/IP, WINS, DHCP, SAMBA, Active Directory, Fax Server
Hardware:	IBM, Sun, HP, Compaq, Dell
Software:	Lotus Notes 4.5 & 5.3, FrontPage, Oracle 7, SMS 1.2 & 2.0, SMS Installer, Wise installer, PVCS, SMS, SMS Installer, Wise installer
Server:	IBM OS/2, Pathworks, Novell Netware, Microsoft NT and 2000
Programming Language:	Basic, Visual Basic, SQL, Oracle, Access, ODBC, VBScript, HTML

Business Experience

FREELANCE CONSULTANT, RALEIGH, NC   2005
- Provided facilitated project planning, project quality and risk assessment to client companies (Gigastorage Corporation and Kaison Corporation) in manufacturing process improvement
- Facilitated process improvement sessions to close gaps between existing and proposed business processes and system architectures. Identified Business Process Re-engineering process modeling support for process improvement initiatives

GLAXOSMITHKLINE INC., RTP, NC   1993 – 2004
Project Manager
- Managed large multi-service infrastructure projects for manufacturing plants in North America.
- Implemented server migration, server consolidation, desktop migration, e-mail migration projects
- Proactively managed business relationships with the business, IT, and Infrastructure teams
- Provided leadership to application and infrastructure development projects and facilitated effective infrastructure planning, budgeting and delivery, day-to-day deployment activities
- 10 years of computer validation experience in the pharmaceutical/product manufacturing industry as it related to GMP, GLP, GCP, and 21 CFR Part 11

APPENDIX – A

Sr. Systems Analyst
- Served as Liaison between clients, technical developers and infrastructure groups
- Managed application development and infrastructure projects
- Implemented full life cycle software development projects and on-going support of various applications written in Visual Basics

Systems Analyst
- Provided application testing on desktop systems, created automated installation scripts for unattended application installation.
- Utilized System Management Server (SMS) for unattended application installs desktop maintenance, security management, and desktop systems optimization.
- Developed detailed systems administration documentation and standards.
- Served as Project Leader on Windows and Exchange migration project in planning and implementing workstation migration to end user communities.

Programmer Analyst
- Managed Pathworks, OS/2 LAN server, NetWare, and Microsoft NT servers for manufacturing staff at RTP and Zebulon sites for over 2000 users.
- Server management activities included performance tuning and capacity planning, server hardware/software maintenance, server and desktop virus and security maintenance, system storage, file security and share management.

INFORMATION SYSTEMS NETWORKS CORPORATION, **RTP, NC**　　　　　　　　　　1991 – 1993

Programmer
- Provided OS/2 workstation and LAN server technical support at IBM RTP site.
- Provided technical and programming support in the area of Local Area Networks management and administration.
- Served as Project Leader on OS/2 migration project in planning and implementing workstation migration to end user communities.

BELL ATLANTIC BUSINESS SYSTEMS SERVICES, INC., Raleigh, NC　　　　　　　　1989 –1991
Software Engineer
- Provided software technical support on desktop applications at Glaxo Inc. Duties included troubleshooting various mainframe and PC applications.
- Supported business applications, Operating systems, terminal emulators, word processors, and database and spreadsheet packages for R&D, Marketing, and Sales Force clients.

RONCO CONSULTING CORPORATION, Durham, NC　　　　　　　　　　　　　　1985 – 1989
Project Coordinator for Near and Far East
- Coordinated and implemented family planning and health improvement projects in Near and Far East under contract with U.S. Agency for International Development (USAID)
- Resident PC specialist administering QNX system/LAN and project databases

Education
M. Ed., Communication Studies, University of North Carolina at Greensboro, Greensboro, NC
B.A., Mass Communications, Tung Hai University, Taichung, Taiwan, the Republic of China

Professional Development
Various certificates in Project Management coursework
Masters Certification in Oracle Database Development

Language
English, Chinese, Japanese (reading)

APPENDIX – A
Richard's Critique of Resume F

✓ The Heading needs to be tightened up and listed on 2 lines.

✓ Eliminate the solid line clear across the page under heading as it could prevent a computer scan in certain software.

✓ The Objective should be targeted and should include the skills the applicant has to offer to support the targeted job.

✓ The Summary of Qualifications includes statements that are not supported in the experience section.

✓ The Computer Skills section only lists what the applicant can do but says nothing about how good they are and, therefore, will not be very helpful to a reviewer. All skills should show level of ability.

✓ Side captions and company names need to be consistent in font size, boldness, and all cap or initial-cap format. The inconsistency shows disorganization and sloppiness.

✓ All of the Work Experience statements are just tasks. None of the statements show what was accomplished in the task.

✓ The experience shown goes back 20 years when only 12-15 years are needed. The applicant needs to be current as systems and technology change so quickly.

✓ The certifications are hidden at the bottom of page 2. Since they support the targeted job, the certifications should be placed right under the Objective with a side caption of "CERTIFICATIONS."

✓ The languages should also be included in the Objective as this could be a differentiator in competition.

✓ The resume includes no outside activities to show the applicant's chemistry.

APPENDIX – A

Resume F After Revisions

LARRY PHIPPS
2733 Wake Forest Way, Wake Forest, NC 27587   (919) 665-xxxx (H)   (919) 512-xxxx (C)   nclp2733@nc.rr.com

OBJECTIVE
IT Project Manager with AlphaVax bringing 13 years of experience in global pharmaceutical industry and skills in strategic planning, client relationship management, system management, and project management. Fluent in Chinese, English, and Japanese.

CERTIFICATION
MCSE, New Horizons, 10/2004
PMP, Wake Tech, 12/2004
Masters Certification in Oracle Database Development, Glaxo Wellcome,   1997

BUSINESS EXPERIENCE
Project Manager - Freelance Consultant   2005
- Facilitated process improvement sessions that closed gaps between existing and proposed business processes and system architectures for client companies.

Project Manager – GlaxoSmithKline (GSK) Inc., RTP, NC   1993 – 2004
- Effectively managed medium-to-large multi-service projects for 13 GSK manufacturing plants in North America with a user base of 8000 and budgets up to $3 million.
- **10 years of excellent computer validation experience in the Pharmaceutical/Product Manufacturing industry as it relates to GMP, GLP, and 21 CFR Part 11.**
- Managed 3 – 20 team members working on application development, infrastructure (server, desktop, operating system, e-mail) migration/upgrade, hardware upgrade/refresh/consolidation technology improvement projects that allowed company to efficiently compete in the pharmaceutical market.
- Deployed creative campaigns that promoted project buy-in to senior management, end users, and technical team members (e-Learning workshops, NetMeeting seminars).
- Developed and implemented marketing strategy that increased user acceptance by 90%.
- **Managed business relationships proactively with business units, IT, and Infrastructure teams that built successful project teams and relationship.**
- Provided leadership to application and infrastructure development projects and facilitated effective planning, budgeting, delivery, and day-to-day deployment activities that resulted in successful projects delivered on time and under budget.
- Led cross-functional teams in computer validation projects following FDA regulations and guidelines that resulted in timely project delivery and avoided product recalls.

Programmer - Information Systems Networks Corporation, RTP, NC   1991 – 1993
- Successfully completed OS/2 workstation and Local Area Network (LAN) migration project to 500 clients.

Also worked as Software Engineer at Bell Atlantic Business Systems and Senior Support Associate and Project Coordinator at government contract firms.

EDUCATION
M.Ed./Communications, University of North Carolina at Greensboro, Greensboro, NC
B.A./Mass Communications, Tung Hai University, Taichung, Taiwan, R.O.C.

LANGUAGE
English, Chinese (Mandarin and Taiwanese), Japanese (reading)

ACTIVITIES
Global trotting, hiking, and watching movies

APPENDIX – A

Larry Phipps Technical Addendum

PHARMACEUTICAL TECHNOLOGY SKILLS

- **10 years of computer validation experience in the Pharmaceutical/Product Manufacturing industry as it relates to GMP, GLP, GCP, and 21 CFR Part 11**
- Pharmaceutical process and product validation on manufacturing processes, FDA rationale, and documentation requirements on pharmaceutical applications - Advanced

PROJECT MANAGEMENT (SAMPLE PROJECTS)

- **Project Manager:** Led cross-functional team with 15 members in server consolidation project from 4 North America sites. Project scope included new server purchase, upgrade, decommission and staff reduction. Resulted in annual saving of $250,000
- **Implementation Project Manager:** Led deployment team of 20 members in workstation and e-mail migration project to 8000 end users in 13 North America sites
- Stream Leader: SAP (supply chain management) for Global Manufacturing and Supply in installing a global ERP system. Led a team of 10 analysts successfully in data migration preparing/ verifying/exporting data from legacy system upload to SAP.

COMPUTER SKILLS

Category	Experience Level	Last Used
Networking		
Novel Netware 4.2 & 5.0	Advanced	Not recently
Windows NT 3.5 & 4.0, XP	Advanced	Current
Windows 2000 server	Advanced	Current
RAS/Terminal server services	Intermediate	Current
Operating Systems		
MS-DOS	Advanced	Current
Windows NT	Advanced	Current
Windows 2000	Advanced	Current
Windows XP	Advanced	Current
UNIX	Knowledgeable	Current
Hardware		
IBM (mainframe, PC, AS/400)	Intermediate	Current
Sun	Knowledgeable	Not recently
HP-UX	Intermediate	Current
Compaq	Intermediate	Current
Dell	Intermediate	Current
Software		
Lotus Notes	Advanced	Current
FrontPage	Intermediate	Current
SMS 1.2, 2.0	Advanced	Current
SMS Installer	Advanced	Current
PVCS	Advanced	Current
Visio 2000	Intermediate	Current
Programming Languages		
HTML	Intermediate	Current
Visual Basic	Intermediate	Not recently
Basic	Intermediate	Not recently
TESTING TOOLS		
QARun	Intermediate	Current
QALoad	Intermediate	Current
DevTrack	Knowledgeable	Not recently

APPENDIX – A

Resume G Before Revisions

MELODY A. DAVIS
800 Gateway Drive
Raleigh, NC 27611

(919) 812-xxxx
mdavis61@aol.com

OBJECTIVE

A challenging and rewarding position in Nursing, utilizing abilities developed through education and experience.

EDUCATION

1981-1983   WAKE TECHNICAL COMMUNITY COLLEGE, Raleigh, NC
Associate Degree in Nursing

1976-1977   CENTRAL PIEDMONT COMMUNITY COLLEGE, Charlotte, NC
Diploma in Medical Office Assisting

Further Professional Training
Basic Life Support – American Heart Association – 1993
Advanced Techniques in Medical Nursing
Basic EKG Interpretation
Basic and Advanced Arrhythmia Course
Numerous in-service courses at Wake Medical Center
Advanced Cardiac Life Support – American Heart Association – 1992
Member of American Association of Critical Care Nurses

Registered Nurse, State of North Carolina – 1983

PROFESSIONAL EXPERIENCE

1985-2005   WAKE MEDICAL CENTER, Raleigh, NC
Registered Nurse
- Coronary Care Unit (CCU)

Responsible for two critically ill cardiac patients.
Monitored cardiac rhythms, pulmonary artery catheters, intra-aortic balloon pump, titrating IV drips and managed ventilated patients.
Functioned in Charge Nurse role requiring supervision of eight to nine nurses, making patient assignments and problem solving. Served as a resource to new employees.
- Telemetry

Responsible for patient care on a 40-bed cardiac monitoring floor.
Performed in Charge Nurse role and cared for patients after PTCA (balloon) procedure.
- Powell Hall

Responsible for patient care on a 39-bed Medical/Surgical Floor. Functioned in Charge Nurse role.

APPENDIX – A

1984-1985   BRITTHAVEN OF RALEIGH, Raleigh, NC
Registered Nurse – Charge Nurse
- Supervised four nursing assistants.

Responsible for patient care including tracheotomy and gastrostomy care, medications, etc.

1982-1984   WAKE MEDICAL CENTER, Raleigh, NC
Registered Nurse
- Responsible for patient care on Medical/Surgical floor.

1979-1981   EASTWAY MEDICAL CLINIC
Certified Medical Assistant
- Assisted doctors with examinations and treatment.
- Served as Medical Secretary, performing routine clerical functions.

1977-1979   CHARLOTTE MEMORIAL HOSPITAL, Charlotte, NC
Certified Medical Assistant
- Responsibilities similar to above.

REFERENCES AVAILABLE UPON REQUEST

APPENDIX – A
Richard's Critique of Resume G

✓ The Objective should be targeted and should include the skills the applicant has to offer to support the targeted job.

✓ The Education statements are not recent and should go at the bottom of the resume. What best supports the targeted Objective (education or experience) should appear right under the Objective.

✓ "Responsible for" statements do not really say what the applicant did. Someone else may have done the work, and the resume needs to say what the applicant accomplished.

✓ Task statements need to describe skills used and the results achieved to show how successful the applicant has been.

✓ Dates go on the far right since what you have done is more important than when it was done.

✓ Do not use "etc." on a resume. The reader has no idea what it means although it implies that you achieved more.

✓ "References available upon request" is not needed as that is a "given."

✓ The resume includes no outside activities to show the applicant's chemistry.

APPENDIX – A

Resume G After Revisions

MELODY A. DAVIS
800 Gateway Drive, Raleigh, NC 27611   (919) 812-xxxx   mdavis61@aol.com

OBJECTIVE
Registered Nurse with Rex Healthcare bringing 15+ years of dedicated experience and skills in coronary, telemetry, medical/surgical, and geriatric care.

LICENSES AND CERTIFICATIONS
Registered Nurse, State of North Carolina
Medical Surgical Nursing Review, RN Refresher Program by UNC Chapel Hill
CPR and BLS Certified

RELATED EXPERIENCE
- **Delivered exceptional care to critically ill patients in Coronary Care Unit that included monitoring of cardiac rhythms, pulmonary artery catheters and intra-aortic balloon pumps, titrating IV drips, and managing ventilated patients.**
- **Coordinated with doctors, nurses, families, and therapists that ensured optimum care for each patient.**

- Educated patient and family members on issues related to the special care needed by critically ill or compromised patients that kept them alert to possible problems.
- **Supervised 8 nurses on telemetry in an alternating role as Charge Nurse making patient assignments, problem solving, telemetry monitoring and interpretation that provided skilled nursing and proper care for all patients.**
- Provided pre- and post-operative care for cardiac catheterization, PTCA, cardioversion, and Pacemaker insertion that kept procedures on schedule.
- Alternated role as Charge Nurse on 39-bed Medical/Surgical Unit and provided supervision that efficiently managed patient care, performed assessments, and administered medications and treatments.
- Managed 4 nursing assistants as Charge Nurse for long-term skilled nursing facility delivering high quality care to geriatric patients that resulted in family members giving thanks for the care their loved ones received.

WORK HISTORY
Staff Nurse/Charge Nurse, Wake Medical Center, Raleigh, NC   10+ years
Charge Nurse, Britthaven of Raleigh, Raleigh, NC   2 years
Certified Medical Office Assistant, Eastway Medical Clinic, Charlotte, NC   2 years
Certified Medical Assistant, Charlotte Memorial Hospital, Charlotte, NC   2 years

EDUCATION
Associate Degree in Nursing, Wake Technical Community College, Raleigh, NC
Diploma in Medical Office Assisting, Central Piedmont Community College, Charlotte, NC

ACTIVITIES
Charity fundraiser
Girl Scout
Mentor children
Aerobics

APPENDIX – A

Resume H Before Revisions

MILTON JEFFREY 701 Wyoming Street, Cary, NC 27501   mjeffrey3@aolcom
(home) 919) 303-xxxx   (cell) (919) 303-xxxx

CAREER OBJECTIVE:
I am seeking a greater challenge of growing sales and profits within the Weyerhaeuser Company. My goal is to be recognized as a top performer in my market.

EMPLOYMENT HISTORY:

Sales & Marketing Manager – Factory Built & Industrial Segment
  May 1996-Jan 2005   **Weyerhaeuser Company** Federal Way, WA Home Office – Cary, NC
Responsible for 6 National Account relationships along with supporting 17 branch sellers in the distribution of Weyerhaeuser produced & outside purchased building products. Sales for my area tripled in 3 years with 20% increase in marginal percent. Other duties included establishing strategic goals, vendor relationship management, market development for new products, pull through sales strategies, and implementing and measuring results. My geographic area is primarily the eastern US with 75% travel. Most recently introduced Lyputs Brazilian hardwood by establishing distributors, OEM accounts, and creating demand with architects.

Sales Manager
  May 1995-May 1996   **Georgia-Pacific**   Raleigh, NC
Responsible for 5 inside & 3 outside sellers of commodity & specialty wood products. Other duties included product management for Eng. Wood Products, inventory replenishment, and component calculations. Sales in the established territory expanded a modest 5%, June 1996, the sales and marketing function relocated to Atlanta, GA

Outside Sales Representative
  Sept 1988-May 1995   **Georgia-Pacific**   Raleigh, NC
Responsible for sales and profits of building materials to OEM accounts in North Carolina. Sales grew from $4 million to $25 million by 1994. The business expanded by creating partnerships with customers while providing valued service.

Inside & Outside Sales Representative
  April 1981-Sept 1988   **Georgia-Pacific**   Houston, TX
Began as an inside seller for Champion International (purchased by GP). I continued my employment as an outside seller of commodity based building products to OEM accounts and retail lumberyards.

EDUCATION:
  1974-1978 **West Virginia University**   Morgantown, WV
   Bachelor's of Science in Business Administration – Marketing
  1994 – Georgia-Pacific Selling Seminar – "Spin Selling"
  1997 – SAMA – Strategic Account Management Association – Annual Convention & Seminar
  2000 – Weyerhaeuser "Value Proposition" Seminar & implementation

PERSONAL SKILLS:
   I am successful in establishing rapport with customers and vendors resulting in obtaining dynamic results. My communication skills, written, oral, and electronic, are strong. My work environment has always included teamwork. I consider myself to be flexible, proactive, ethical, and results driven. I embrace change with positive enthusiasm. I believe in planning for success, implementing tactics, and measuring results. Providing value and customer service is paramount. I have a great working knowledge of Microsoft computer programs Excel, Word, and PowerPoint. I have a safe and clean driving record.

PERSONAL DATA:
  Married (21 years) with one child in college, excellent health.

APPENDIX – A
Richard's Critique of Resume H

✓ Resumes are written in third person. The applicant should not use "I", "me," or "my."

✓ The Career Objective is too personal and general. Objective needs to include a targeted job, targeted company, and the experience and skills the applicant can bring to that position.

✓ Job information goes on one line and should state job title (bold), company name, location, and dates.

✓ Dates go on the far right since what you have done is more important than when it was done.

✓ "Responsible for" and "other duties" statements don't say what the applicant did. These statements usually come from job descriptions and state what the person was supposed to do. The resume needs to state what the applicant actually did.

✓ This resume includes company information (relocations and name changes) that need to be eliminated. The resume is about you.

✓ The Experience section needs task statements to start with "bulleted" action words. The paragraph format tends to blend information and the most important item may be last and never read.

✓ Personal skills and personal thoughts should go in the cover letter, not on the resume.

✓ Personal data does not go on a resume.

✓ Important points need to be made bold to guide the reader's eyes in a 30-second review.

✓ "&" looks like it has been used to save space. This little figure takes one digit and "and" takes only 3 digits. Using "&" repeatedly makes you look lazy.

✓ The resume includes no outside activities to show the applicant's chemistry.

APPENDIX – A

Resume H After Revisions

MILTON JEFFREY
701 Wyoming Street, Cary, NC 27501   (h) 919) 303-xxxx   (c) (919) 303-xxxx   mjeffrey3@aolcom

OBJECTIVE
Technical Sales Representative with Brooks Building Products bringing 15+ years of successful sales and marketing experience and skills in generating new accounts and increasing existing accounts in the building materials field.

RELATED WORK EXPERIENCE

Sales and Marketing Manager, Weyerhaeuser Company, Cary, NC   1996-2005
- **Tripled sales in 4 years with a 20% increase in gross margin by expanding product mix with existing and new customers in the factory built segment.**
- **Generated new sales to a major national account that resulted in $4 million annually for 4 consecutive years for a strategic company produced product.**

- Tripled sales in one year and increased gross margin by 36% by providing value-added services to a four location industrial account.
- Increased sales by $1 million annually with above average margins in the factory built segment by developing a new product source for a roofing accessory requested by key customers.
- Led two sub-segment strategic planning sessions for the industrial market that could aggressively double sales for 2004.
- Generated over 50 sales leads while managing trade show activities by introducing two new products for the factory built segment.

Sales Manager, Georgia-Pacific, Raleigh, NC   1988-1996
- **Increased sales in territory from $4 million to $25 million in 5 years by building new relationships with 18 OEM accounts in North Carolina.**
- Exceeded sales quota by $2 million managing 5 inside and 2 outside sellers that targeted new and existing customers.
- Managed the replenishment of engineered wood product line that exceeded the strategic plans in inventory returns and obsolete items by year's end.

Also was successful as an outside sales representative for Champion International in Houston, TX.

EDUCATION
BA/Business Administration/Marketing, West Virginia University, Morgantown, WV

ACTIVITIES
Sports enthusiast
Mentor children

APPENDIX – A

Resume I Before Revisions

Paul R. Simmons
409 Sandy Walk Drive
Raleigh, N.C. 27615
919-870-xxxx
simmonspr@aol.com

OBJECTIVE
Software position utilizing strengths in problem solving and analysis of intricate software systems.

SUMMARY OF QUALIFICATIONS
Extensive software engineering experience in complex real-time systems. Quick learner, with ability to adapt to rapidly changing project demands. Special talent for seeing the big picture and quickly solving tough problems with excellence and innovation. Proven expertise in:

- Embedded software development
- Object-oriented software development
- Results-oriented problem solving
- Strategic software feature planning
- Real-time software development
- Leadership / Team development
- Consulting / Coaching
- Teaching / Training / Mentoring

TECHNICAL SKILLS
- Languages: C / C++, C#, Java, HTML,ML,JavaScript, Assembly (80x86, 8085,8051), SL-1
- Operating Systems: UNIX, Windows, PSOS, MTOS, RMX
- Communications Protocols: TCP / IP, SS7, ISDN Q.931 and Q.932, ATM, H.248
- Communications Interfaces: Ethernet, SONET, T1, RS-232, RS-422, RS-488
- Tools: Dreamweaver,Excel,FrameMaker+SGML, PowerPoint, Rational ClearCase, Word

PROFESSIONAL EXPERIENCE
Nortel Networks, Research Triangle Park, North Carolina   **1994-2005**
Software Engineer / Media Gateway Development – Succession Networks **2000-2005**
Developed C++ object-oriented call processing software for Voice over Internet Protocol (VoIP) and Voice over Asynchronous Transfer Mode (ATM) solutions on a Media Gateway.
- Delivered call processing software on time, in an environment of rapidly changing project requirements. This included 20 % additional functionality that was not originally scheduled.
- Created integration test plan for call processing interface to maintenance and data base subsystems, which kept project on schedule. Led review of test plan document, and executed all test cases relating to call processing subsystem.

Software Engineer / Team Leader – DMS-10 Development   1994-1999
Designed and integrated new features into eight million lines of existing code for DMS-10, a digital telephone switch, with an installed base of 5,000 worldwide. Each release contributed over $100M in revenue.
- Received 1998 Nortel Technical Services Symposium Award for most outstanding presentation based on customer feedback.

APPENDIX – A

- Developed billing software for Local Number Portability (LNP), a feature that permits a subscriber to change local service provider and retain their telephone number, as part of initial design team. Devised a method to reuse customers' existing large digit translations database, significantly reducing cost of ownership. Resulted in multi-million dollar contracts with all major U.S. telephone companies. Promoted to LNP team leader.
- Acted as LNP Consultant and subject expert for three years, including strategic feature planning. Consulted for marketing, technical support, sales engineering, customer training, customer service, and directly with customers, resulting in 40 % increase in customer satisfaction.
- Led three-person team that developed and modified software to resolve issues related to local ten-digit dialing, resulting in 15 % increase in customer satisfaction.
- Recognized serious missing functionality in LNP software, convinced senior management of problem, and developed software that resolved deficiency. Resulted in a major customer contract.
- Researched problem found by a customer. Determined it was an industry-wide problem, and devised a unique solution. Worked with technical support and customer to test solution.
- Championed development of number pooling software, a feature that helps conserve availability of new telephone numbers. Led team that developed appropriate software, resulting in a $3 million dollar contract with a major telephone company.
- Designed and developed billing software for ISDN Basic Rate Interface (BRI) release.

Aerotek, Reading, Pennsylvania   **1993**
Software Engineer
Developed embedded maintenance software for a Digital Cross Connect system, using C, TCP/IP, Ethernet and PSOS kernel.

Alcatel Network Systems, Raleigh, North Carolina   **1991-1992**
Software Engineer / Team Leader
Designed and developed embedded Network Management software for a SONET (Synchronous Optical Network) OC3 Add/Drop Multiplexer. Used C and MTOS real-time kernel.

Rockwell Electronic Commerce, Wood Dale, Illinois   **1985-1991**
Software Engineer
Developed embedded Digital Loop Carrier software using C, 8086 assembly and RMX kernel.

Fox Valley Software, Batavia, Illinois   **1984-1985**
Software Design Engineer
Developed maintenance and diagnostic software at AT&T Bell Labs for 5ESS digital telephone switching system using C and UNIX software development tools.

Teradyne, Inc., Deerfield, Illinois   **1982-1984**
Software Applications Engineer
Developed embedded maintenance and diagnostic software for a Subscriber Loop Testing system. Included customization of software at client sites. Used C and 8085 assembly.

Rockwell Electronic Commerce, Wood Dale, Illinois   **1980-1982**
Software Engineer
Developed software to test an Automatic Call Distributor telephone system using 8085 assembly.

Northrop Corporation, Rolling Meadows, Illinois   **1979-1980**
Hardware Engineer
Designed interface hardware for Automated Test Equipment. Held a Secret security clearance.

EDUCATION
BS, Computer Engineering, University of Illinois at Urbana Champaign, Urbana, Illinois   1979
Eta Kappa Nu, National Electrical Engineering Honor Society

PROFESSIONAL DEVELOPMENT
Object Oriented Languages and Systems, Computer Science 517, North Carolina State University
C# - Tech Engage - March, 2003; Working on Network+ Certification;
Training on CGI, Perl, PHP, MySQL and MS Access 2002

APPENDIX – A
Richard's Critique of Resume I

- ✓ The Objective does not show the amount of experience and is short on skills.

- ✓ The Summary of Qualifications includes statements that are not supported in the experience section. Personal characteristics belong in the cover letter.

- ✓ The Technical skills section contains only lists and should include the level of ability for each to help a reviewer. A Technical Addendum would help.

- ✓ The Professional Experience section includes a general description of each job plus bulleted statements that are sometimes paragraphs, but do include results with most of the statements. Do not use paragraphs. Results, if included, in paragraphs are at the end and may not get read.

- ✓ The resume includes the applicant's complete work history, although skimpy, for the older jobs. Only the last 12-15 years need to be included on an advertisement resume.

- ✓ The Certification program that the applicant is pursuing is buried under Professional Development.

- ✓ The resume includes no outside activities to show the applicant's chemistry.

APPENDIX – A

Resume I After Revisions

Paul R. Simmons
409 Sandy Walk Drive, Raleigh, NC 27615 (919) 870-xxxx <u>simmonspr@aol.com</u>

OBJECTIVE
Senior Software Engineer with IBM bringing 15+ years of experience and excellent skills in embedded real-time and object-oriented software development, results-oriented problem solving, and strategic software feature planning.

CERTIFICATION
Network+, Wake Technical Community College, Raleigh, NC (Expected 3/2005)

RELATED EXPERIENCE
Senior Software Engineer, Nortel Networks, RTP, NC 1994 to 2005
- Delivered C++ object-oriented call processing software on time for Voice over Internet Protocol (VOIP) telephone switching equipment that resulted in 20 % additional functionality not originally scheduled.

- Developed key software modules for Local Number Portability (LNP) feature that resulted in at least 8 multi-million dollar contracts.
- Served as LNP Consultant and subject expert for 3 years, including strategic feature planning, with marketing, sales, technical support, sales engineering, customer service, and directly with customers, that answered many questions and solved many problems.
- Championed and led development team for Number Pooling software that resulted in a $3 million contract.

Senior Software Engineer, Aerotek, Reading, PA 1993
- Developed embedded maintenance software for a telephone transmission system, using C, TCP/IP, Ethernet and PSOS real-time operating system (OS), and personally redesigned voice processing software with zero defects and 25% increase in speed of execution.

Senior Software Engineer, Alcatel Network Systems, Raleigh, NC 1991 to 1992
- Designed and developed embedded Network Management software for a fiber-optic telephone transmission system that interacted with several different external network management systems, on time and with zero defects.

Also worked as software engineer for Rockwell Electronic Corp., Fox Valley Software, and Teradyne, Inc. and as a hardware engineer for Northrop Grumman Corporation, all in Illinois.

EDUCATION
BS/Computer Engineering, University of Illinois at Urbana Champaign

ACTIVITIES
Volunteer coach, YMCA
Mentoring children

Paul R. Simmons

Technical Addendum

Category	Experience Level	Last Used
Programming Languages		
C	Expert	Recently
C++	Advanced	Recently
Java / J2EE	Intermediate	Recently
8086 Assembly	Expert	Not Recently
Database Systems		
Oracle	Knowledgeable	Recently
Access 2000	Knowledgeable	Recently
Web Technologies		
HTML	Knowledgeable	Recently
XML	Knowledgeable	Recently
JSP	Knowledgeable	Recently
Servlets	Knowledgeable	Recently
MySQL	Knowledgeable	Recently
PHP 4.0	Knowledgeable	Recently
Selected Applications		
Dreamweaver MX	Knowledgeable	Recently
MS Office applications	Intermediate	Recently
Framemaker+SGML	Intermediate	Recently
Rational ClearCase	Expert	Recently
Operating Systems		
Windows	Intermediate	Recently
UNIX	Advanced	Recently
PSOS	Advanced	Not Recently
VxWorks	Advanced	Not Recently
Communications Protocols		
TCP / IP	Intermediate	Recently
ATM	Intermediate	Recently
SS7	Expert	Recently
Communication Interfaces		
Ethernet	Advanced	Recently
SONET	Advanced	Recently
T1	Advanced	Recently

APPENDIX – A
Resume J Before Revisions

Ralph T. Young

7231 Crystal Blue St
Apex, NC 27507

Home: 919-602-xxxx
E-mail: youngrt@nc.rr.com

Wanted Position: Verification Engineer

Skills:
- Extensive experience in product verification, customer acceptance testing, product field trials and all stages of the product development life cycle.
- Extensive experience in functional and system level testing of telecom and networking products.
- Working knowledge in: Requirements management, design and verification processes, fault tracking, quality metrics and ISO 9001.
- Excellent leadership and communication skills.

Software & Technical Skills:

PC Applications: Microsoft Office Suite, MS Project, MS Outlook, FrontPage 2000, ClearQuest, Quick Books Pro
Languages: PLEX, PASCAL, Assembly, ERLANG
Operating Systems: Windows 98/NT/2000/XP, UNIX
Protocols: Bluetooth™, ANSI41, TCP/IP, ISDN, IS-136,
Recent training in: C++, JAVA, GSM/GPRS

Education:
University of Texas at Dallas
B.S., Business Administration, June 1991
Major Concentration in Management Information Systems
Cum Laude Graduate – GPA 3.95/4.0

R.E.T.S Electronic Institute, Birmingham, Alabama
A.A.S., Electronic Engineering Technology, May 1981

Work Experience:

Ericsson Inc., (May / 1991 – Present)
Verification Engineer, Research Triangle Park, NC (8/02 – present)
- Lead verification engineer responsible for testing of Bluetooth™ protocol on SonyEricsson CDMA mobile phones.
- Responsible for tracking compliance with Bluetooth™ version 1.1 specification
- Work closely with the design team to identify and resolve Bluetooth™ related issues.

Verification Project Leader, Research Triangle Park, NC (9/98 – 7/02)
- Verification Project Leader for the Digital Wireless Office project (12,000 man-hour). Responsible for verification project planning, project schedule and budget.
- Key player in obtaining product certification for Ericsson's Digital Wireless Office product from AT&T Wireless.

Resource and Competence Manager, Ericsson Inc., Richardson, TX (9/97-9/98)
- Managed a group of 26 verification engineers.
- Resource planning for design & verification projects, evaluation of employee performance and employee recruiting.

Verification Project Leader, Ericsson Inc., Richardson, TX (1/97 – 10/97)
- Verification Project Leader for a Local Number Portability project (25,000 man-hour). Responsible for planning and monitoring project schedule and costs. Overall planning, control and coordination of verification activities.
- Coordinated system verification activities, weekly customer status meetings, Bellcore acceptance testing, First Office Application planning and support.

APPENDIX – A

System Test Leader, Ericsson Inc., Richardson, TX (6/93 – 12/96)
- System Test Leader for AIN 0.1 verification project (20,000 man-hour). Performed test analysis, planning, scheduling, evaluation and progress reporting.
- Test Leader for 5 separate Telecom Switching projects, which included the introduction of newly designed SW & HW.

Software Integration Engineer, Ericsson Inc., Richardson, TX (6/91 – 6/93)
Responsible for creation and debugging of software test environments for Class 5 Telecom switching systems used for Verification activities.

Siemens Public Switching, Boca Raton, FL (9/84 – 7/88)
Member of the Technical Staff
- Installed and maintained digital telecommunication switches in the software verification lab.
- New project coordinator and liaison between hardware design project in Munich Germany and local software design and verifications group.
- Designed, wrote and implemented database software to track HW inventory and ordering process.

Mitel Corp., Boca Raton FL (6/81 – 9/84)
Product Engineering Technician
- Worked as subject matter expert providing technical product support and guidance to manufacturing team on the Mitel PBX equipment.
- Coordinated the deployment of design changes into the manufacturing process. Monitored product integrity throughout the production process.

References available upon request

APPENDIX – A
Richard's Critique of Resume J

✓ An Objective should be used instead of "Wanted Position." The Objective shows what you have to offer, not what you want.

✓ The Skills section lists only what the applicant can do but says nothing about how good he is and, therefore, will not be very helpful to a reviewer. All skills should show level of ability.

✓ The list of Software and Technical Skills does not show level of ability.

✓ The Education section is misplaced. If the applicant is getting the next job based on work experience, the Education section goes down to the bottom of the resume.

✓ Under Education, the school, degree, and major should all go on one line.

✓ Under Work Experience, the job title (bold), company, location, and dates should all go on one line.

✓ Instead of using 6 job titles, show the top title and include anything you did for that company that supports the experience and skills you have to offer to the potential employer. Add a couple of bulleted statements to show other skills you can offer.

✓ "Responsible for" statements are not useful. They show only what you were supposed to do, not what you actually did.

✓ All of the Work Experience statements are just tasks. None of the statements show what was accomplished in the task.

✓ Work statements should start with action verbs.

✓ "References available upon request" is not needed as that is a "given."

✓ The resume includes no outside activities to show the applicant's chemistry.

APPENDIX – A

Resume J After Revisions

RALPH T. YOUNG

7231 Crystal Blue St
Apex, NC 27507

919-602-xxxx
youngrt@nc.rr.com

OBJECTIVE
Verification Engineer with Company XYZ bringing 15+ years of engineering experience and proven skills in product verification, certification, customer acceptance activities, new product field trials, and customer support.

EXPERIENCE
Senior Verification Engineer, Ericsson Inc., Various locations 13 years

- **Achieved the first successful certification of the Bluetooth™ protocol on SonyEricsson CDMA mobile phones as the primary verification engineer on the Bluetooth design feature team.**

- **Obtained product certification for Ericsson's Digital Wireless Office System from AT&T Wireless by performing product demonstrations and supporting customer acceptance activities that enabled Ericsson to promptly enter a new market.**
- Directed all verification activities for a 25,000 man-hour Local Number Portability project including: functional and system level testing, Bellcore™ compliance testing, customer acceptance testing and new product field trials that enabled Ericsson, and their customers, to meet regulatory deadlines for implementation of this service.
- Planned, scheduled, monitored and initiated corrective action for system test activities on several networking projects that resulted in the successful introduction of new hardware and software to existing platforms.
- Utilized engineering skills and experience to rapidly obtain expertise of new technology that was a key factor to the success of several projects.
- Debugged software and created software patches for critical faults that allowed the verification process to continue and maintain the project schedule.

Also worked with testing and problem solving as a Technical Engineer and Product Engineering Technician for Siemens Public Switching and Mitel Corp. in FL.

EDUCATION
BS/Business Administration/MIS, University of Texas at Dallas
Cum Laude graduate with major concentration in Management Information Systems

AAS/EE Technology, RETS Electronic Institute, Birmingham, AL

ACTIVITIES
Camping
Fishing
Golf

APPENDIX – A

RALPH T. YOUNG

Technical Addendum

Category	Experience Level	Last Used
Test Equipment		
PreQual Bluetooth Tester	Expert	Current
Merlin Tracer/Trainer	Intermediate	Current
MGTS	User	1998
Protocols		
ANSI41	Intermediate	2002
TCP/IP	User	Current
ISDN	Intermediate	2002
IS-136	Intermediate	2002
Programming Languages		
PASCAL	Intermediate	1994
Assembly	Intermediate	1998
PLEX	Advanced	1998
JAVA	Beginner	2004
C++	Beginner	2003
Visual Basic	Beginner	2003
Operating Systems		
Windows NT/2000/XP	Intermediate	Current
UNIX	User	2003
Selected Applications		
Clear Quest	Intermediate	Current
Rational Test Manager	User	Current
MS Office Applications	Advanced	Current
MS Project	Intermediate	Current
FrontPage 2000 / HTML	Intermediate	Current
Photoshop	User	Current
Quick Books Pro	Intermediate	Current
Wireless Platforms		
TDMA	Intermediate	2001
GSM	Intermediate	2001
Bluetooth	Intermediate	Current
802.11a	Intermediate	2001

APPENDIX – B

The Background on Book and Layout

In **Make Your Resume Talk**, we give you guidelines to help you write and re-write your advertisement resume in segments. An advertising resume describes your experience and skills and shows how good you are in those skills. It is different because most resumes are the basic obituary resume that just describes your tasks and doesn't give any indication of how good you are. Some resumes show an achievement section, but when closely read they are just tasks. The purpose of this approach is for you to visualize and build a successful resume that you will be proud of when you finish so you can get interviews.

It is like building a house. First, you have an idea, then a blueprint, then you start building the structure from the ground up, and then you are proud when it is all finished. The resume process is the same. First, you have a job you want to apply for; then you have to follow an outline to tailor your experience and skills to that job; then you have to go through the Heading, Objective, Work Experience, Education, and Activities sections; and then you need to be proud of how you advertised your experience and skills on a piece of paper.

The instruction starts with the heading and gives different options of how to write it until you find one that fits you. The instruction continues through the Objective, Work Experience, Computer Skills, Education, and Activities providing guidelines and examples of what to include and how to write each section. If you don't like what you wrote, you will want to go back and re-read the guidelines, and then you can make the necessary changes to **Make Your Resume Talk** for you.

Remember, your objective is to explain what you really did and how good you are. Therefore, your resume must include the proper information to "talk for you" so you can get the interviews you desire. The resume is an advertisement of your experience and skills and what you have to offer a potential employer. At the interview, you will have to re-sell your experience and skills. Having thought about what you have done and how good you are for your advertisement resume, you should be well prepared to sell yourself in the interview.

The "before and after" examples in this book are just examples to illustrate how resumes can be changed from an obituary resume to an advertisement resume. The "after" resumes were primarily from former students or clients, used with their approval, who got interviews after making the suggested changes shown in the critiques. My only warning is for you to tailor your experience and skills to each specific job and don't blindly copy statements from these examples.

APPENDIX – B

Background on book

Dick Hart has reviewed thousands of resumes and talked to recruiters, Human Resources managers, business executives, and various employers to get a better understanding of what makes a resume **talk.** He has also received feedback from students on their reactions from using the advertisement approach taught in this book. Based on this information and the author's own beliefs of a practical way to write a resume that gets read, **he has prepared this insightful, informative, results-oriented information on how to move your resume to the top of the stack and keep it out of "file 13."**

What do employers look for in a resume? What makes them read past a 30-second glance to find the skills the applicant could bring to their company? These are questions the author tried to find answers for. He found that the Objective was the key and must show the experience and skills the applicant has to offer a potential employer. He also found that results were not included with the tasks in the Work Experience section. Finally, most books eliminated Activities as an essential part of the resume. Mr. Hart didn't agree: he thinks activities show the chemistry of the person.

Frustrated at the lack of practical, easy-to-read information on how to visualize and write an advertisement resume, the author developed the information in this book to help individuals prepare a resume that they could be proud of and could **talk** for them to anyone who reviewed it. He has tried to make the information basic and easy to read with examples to support the way each section should be written. The "after" examples show how to say something worth reading and **Make Your Resume Talk.**

Mr. Hart taught his first class at Wake Technical Community College in Raleigh, NC, in 2001 and focused on specific-job targeting, results and achievements to show how good the applicant's skills were, and the successes achieved in prior jobs. Students asked, "How do you know your approach to resumes is the right way?" The author went out to businesses in the Raleigh area to see what made employers read a resume and what made them throw resumes away. Employers sometimes receive over 1,000 resumes for one job, so it is imperative to have a resume that shows:

◆ **What you have done,**
◆ **How good you are, and**
◆ **That these results can talk to the reader.**

Remember, the employer usually gives the resume a quick 30-second review, so the resume better **talk** for you.

The businesses visited included a cross section of jobs including skilled trades, computer and engineering companies, retail establishments, and service industries, as well as human resource companies (recruiters). The feedback was clear and distinct - make the resumes short and describe your tasks and skills with results that jump out to entice the reviewer to read more than the initial 30-second review. The information obtained in this research supported the author's own feelings about resumes.

Many former students have sent e-mail messages back to the college attributing their refocused results-oriented resume for their success in getting an interview and a job.

This success led to the publication of this book. Many of the testimonials are shown in the appropriate chapters of the book to illustrate the impact of how writing results-oriented statements helped applicants in the interviews to land challenging positions. Other testimonials are shown on the next page.

APPENDIX – C

Testimonials

"Of all the work I did over 19 weeks of unemployment, nothing compares to what Dick Hart did to empower me to get interviews and find a job. I used the guidelines in his book and ended up with an outstanding resume and an increased confidence for selling myself to potential employers. Let me give you some statistics."

Pre-Dick Hart guidelines
- 15 weeks
- 136 job application resumes
- 3 interviews (.02%)
- 0 offers

Post-Dick Hart Guidelines
- 4 weeks
- 13 job application resumes
- 2 interviews (15.4%)
- 1 offer
- 2 potential interviews/offers
- Back to work

Mel Miller
Computer Design Engineer

"Tens of thousands of resumes are thrown away every day because they don't say anything or are so poorly written they never get a chance to speak. Dick Hart's advice helped me and many others I know personally to do it right, get the interview, and land the job. This is essential reading for serious jobseekers."
Lawrence Lytle
Executive Director
World Trade Center North Carolina

"Can your resume talk? Mine didn't, but now it does thanks to Dick Hart.

"After reading through his book, I thought this guy didn't know what he was talking about. But my opinion changed when I decided to follow his instructions. When I re-read my original resume closely, I realized that my resume didn't say anything good about me, which resulted in no responses, not even one, nothing, nil. With my new advertisement resume following his guidelines, I now receive at least one interview each week and this week got two interviews and two-call back interviews."

"So would I say, "Does my resume talk?" Yes, mine does and I highly recommend anyone who wants results to follow his guidelines."
Maryann Smith
Administrative Assistant

"I just went to work as an IT security engineer. Dick Hart's resume guidelines from his book and class clearly made a difference and I can actually say that I wouldn't have got this job had I not been committed to following his advice. In addition to a nice salary, I also got a signing bonus in a tight economical time."

"Although Dick Hart's resume approach may be bold and unusual—they are powerful and they work—for those who are committed and willing to do the hard work that it takes a good employer to see value."
Tim Mongan
IT Security Engineer

APPENDIX – D

Why I wrote This Book !

My name is **Richard Hart** and I'd like to explain why I wrote this book. I was director of training for a large government agency, retired, and became an instructor at Wake Technical Community College in North Carolina in October, 2001. I now teach a course entitled **Make Your Resume Talk.** During my career, I've seen and critiqued thousands of resumes and have first-hand knowledge of which ones are truly effective. The good resumes **"talk"** to the hiring personnel and say, **"Interview Me!"**

Students told me:
1. I'm losing my home because I can't make my mortgage payments after losing my job.
2. I'm a recent graduate and my resume doesn't seem to be getting any attention.
3. I'm going through a divorce because I can't support my family after losing my job.
4. I paid a lot of money to get a resume prepared but got no responses.
5. I heard I had an obituary resume; how do I fix it?
6. I've never written a resume before; what do I need to say?

Many students said they came to class because they heard that I could help them write a better resume, a resume that could talk for them. The mental state of these students and their families challenged me to make a difference in their lives by giving them a resume that will speak for them when read.

I accepted the challenge to help these students so they could get back to work and get their lives back in order. The biggest problem was to get students to realize that their current resumes were not being read and were not ever going to be read in their current format. I emphasized that these students had to re-think who they were and learn to describe how good they were. Many said they were results-oriented people on their resume, but they listed no results. What were recruiters and human resources personnel going to think about them when there was no support for their statements? The resume was already on its way to the trash can.

The best phone calls or e-mail messages that I get are the ones from former students who say "Thank you, I just got a job." My emotions run high when this happens because I have made a positive difference in another person's - and their family's - life. The challenge of helping and the positive feedback pushed me to prepare a course of instruction to teach the ways to write a resume that will get read.

I firmly believe that if you follow the tips and guidelines presented in this book, you can truly Make Your Resume Talk for you and get you interviews and a job.

APPENDIX – D

This book emphasizes the need to write a resume that targets each job opportunity and presents your skills and achievements against the specific requirements of each position. A targeted resume begins with a targeted Objective (headline) that addresses your experience related to a specific job, a targeted company, and presents the experience and skills you can offer to that company. You will find that this style ensures that your resume will be read and get you more interviews. It is not a game of "buzz words"; it is an honest description of statements that tell your story of the skills you can offer to a potential employer and how good you will be for this job. The process of building your resume also emphasizes including your Activities on the resume because they say something about who you really are. Many students have given me feedback saying they got an interview primarily because of something listed in the Activities section that interested the reviewer. You will hear many stories describing why individuals get interviews, but adding activities and other tips that are included in this book will **help you build a resume that will talk for you.**

This book also includes many examples of how to write each section of the resume and includes space to draft each section of your resume after reading the examples. It also includes "before and after" examples, with critiques of the former resumes that will help you to see the changes necessary to make the resumes more positive and effective.

There is no magic in writing an effective resume.

It requires planning and effort,

but the results of a well-written, targeted resume

that talks for you will be worth the effort.

Start now, accept the challenge, and build a resume

that will get you interviews!

APPENDIX – E

Acknowledgements

At the urging of his students, Dick Hart changed the name of this, his second, book to a more positive one because it had such an impact on their lives.

His first book was titled **Can Your Resume Talk?**

This book is entitled **Make Your Resume Talk**.

It contains much more detail and a different format to make it easier for the reader and user to visualize and write an advertisement resume.

The thanks for this book and its direction and approach go to students who bought into the guidelines in the first book but wanted to see it go further. Thus, they became his Book Committee. They, and others that played a key part in the production of this book, are:

- ▶ Mary Brady, a Human Resources Development Coordinator at Wake Technical Community College who ran the resume classes and provided support and contact with unemployment agencies and individuals who took the class.
- ▶ Bill Campbell, a marketing specialist who had success in both sales and marketing and provided help in how to best write and market this information.
- ▶ Jim Dean, former editor of *Wildlife in North Carolina*, who cautiously reviewed every word and provided valuable insight into presentations to continually visualize progress in writing and re-writing resumes in order to produce a resume that each student liked and felt confident to send to potential employers.
- ▶ Ken Dillo, Director of the Small Business Center at Wake Technical Community College and a constant pusher for me to take the big step in the resume business because of the positive impact **Make Your Resume Talk** would have on individuals seeking employment.
- ▶ Darryl Goebel, a former CEO, business owner, and computer guru who provided insight into how to use the Internet to get the message to students and others needing help with their resumes and pushed to use the word "make" instead of "can" as part of the title.
- ▶ Jeff Rizzo, **"The Designer"** a passionate and tireless computer analyst and manager who is certified in many hardware, software, and application areas. His background in desktop publishing was *critical* in helping me produce the book, cover design and Hart's tips artwork.
- ▶ John Teague helped edit this book and is available to help others with award-winning writing and editing for print and online publications. Contact him at john@handmademarketing.com.
- ▶ Pat Ten Eyck, a graphic design specialist who provided the sketches and drawings to emphasize key points in the book.
- ▶ Joan Zimmer, an operations manager who believed in the approach and provided common sense and practical counseling that kept the project on track.

APPENDIX – F

About the Author

RICHARD A. HART

PO Box 563, Holly Springs, NC 27540　　　(919) 222-XXXX　　　rhart21@XXXX.com

OBJECTIVE

Author for Hart's Resumes, Inc. bringing 6 years of passionate and dedicated experience and skills in teaching, counseling, writing, and re-writing resumes that get students interviews and job offers.

RELATED EXPERIENCE

Instructor/Counselor, Wake Technical CC, Raleigh, NC　　　present

- **Taught over 3,000 students (ages 20-76) how to re-think what they have on their obituary resumes and write honest advertisement resumes that make their resume talk and then get job interviews and offers for employment.**
- Accepted challenge to help students get jobs that resulted in research of employer's skill needs and passed information on to students having matching skills.
- **Provide one-on-one counseling sessions and work with students, their resumes, and cover letters that ensure resumes advertise skills and results that match targeted job requirements for a job they will enjoy getting up for each morning.**
- Develop network groups for each class that provides awareness of jobs and support to prepare resumes, apply and get interviews.

Instructor/Supporter, 2 unemployed groups in VA and NC　　　3 years

- **Provided one-on-one instruction in resume preparation and interviewing that helped unemployed members get interviews and job offers.**

OTHER EXPERIENCE

Director of Training/AD for Auditing, General Accounting Office, Wash., DC　　15+ years

- **Provided resume assistance and practice interviews for all exiting employees for a 3-year period that prepared employees to be ready to move to other employment.**
- Testified before Congressional committees after auditing various federal programs that resulted in legislative changes and recommendations to improve specific programs.
- Directed professional and administrative training programs that developed skills to help auditors and clerical employees advance in the Office.

EDUCATION

BS/Accounting, West Virginia Institute of Technology, Montgomery, WV
Varsity basketball and baseball (4 years each)　　Student Government President

COMPUTER SKILLS

Intermediate in Word and Internet.
Knowledgeable in Excel, Quicken, and PowerPoint.

ACTIVITIES

Golf, Spectator sports, Alumni people finder/organizer, Mentor children

Author of "Can Your Resume Talk?"
Author of "Make Your Resume Talk"

INDEX

Abbreviations	96	
Action verbs	17, 20-21	
Advertisement resume	i-ii	
Activities	35-38, 54	
Applications	48	
Apprenticeship	32	
Attachments	99	
Awards and honors	41	
Author	157	
Background on book	151-152	
Bold	iii, 12, 96	
Certificates/Certifications	42	
Changing careers	67-76, 108	
Changing careers resumes		
Manufacturing to Clinical	72-75	
Policeman to Sales	68-71	
Checklist	109	
Chemistry	35, 37	
College graduates	51-66	
College resumes	55-66	
Computer engineer	55-57	
Computer intern	64-66	
Electrical engineer	58-60	
Math teacher/Coach	61-63	
Computer scans	23	
Computer skills	27-30, 47, 53	
Cover letter	89-94, 107	
Basic	92	
Changing careers	71, 90	
Comparing your qualifications		
To the job Requirements	93-94	
Critiques	56, 59, 62, 65, 69, 73, 80, 85, 112, 115, 119, 123, 127, 131, 136, 139, 143, 148	
Dates	15-17	
Education	31-34, 45-46	
Electronic resume	99-104	
Employability	105-106	
Energy	46	
Feedback	iv, 17, 22-23, 35, 37, 144, 154	
Font type / size	95	
Frequently asked		
Questions	107-108	
GED	48	

Hart's Tips	vi, 8, 11-12, 15-18, 22-23, 27-28, 31, 35, 41, 44, 47, 89, 96, 99	
Heading	7-10	
High school resume	45-50	
Honesty	22	
Incomplete education	32, 48	
Internship	53	
Interview yourself	19	
Job titles	15	
Justification	95	
Key points on a resume	iii-iv	
Keywords/buzz words	23, 41, 155	
Languages	46	
Leadership activities	45	
Licenses	42	
Longer resumes	107-108	
Margin settings	95	
Memberships	41	
Mental ability	45	
Military service	39-40	
Mistakes	96	
Name	7	
Obituary resume	2, 3-6	
Objective	1, 3, 11-12, 52	
Old experience	23-24	
One page	97	
Optional items	41-42	
Paper type / color	95	
Persistence	46	
Personal services	108	
Phone message	8	
Physical attributes		
of resume	95-98	
Physical condition	47	
Portfolio	48	

References	43-44	
Reminders	9, 14, 26, 29, 34, 38	
Results	18, 22-23	
Resume examples		
Accounts receivable		
Manager	110-113	
Administrative assistant	114-116	
Clinical research		
Associate	74-75	
Coach	86-87	
Controller	117-121	
Environmental technician	122-124	
Marketing manager	125-128	
Nurse	134-137	
Personal assistant/Nanny	78-80	
Project manager – IT	129-133	
Sales	138-140	
Software engineer	141-146	
Special education		
Teacher	88	
Verification engineer	146-150	
Resume format	33	
Resume struggles	1	
Resume preparation	95-97	
Return to earlier job	77-81	
Return to workforce	90	
Reverse-chronological		
Resume	16, 67, 77, 83	
Rule of thumb	iii, 2	
Salary history	90	
Salary requirements	90	
Shotgun approach	107	
Special skills	48	
Spell check	96	
Standard resume		
E-Resume example	103-104	
Stay-at-home Mom	24, 81	
Summary	41	
Tailor your resume	83-88, 107	
Targeted Objective	11-14, 52	
Technical addendum	27-28, 53, 75, 121, 133, 145, 150	
Testimonials	153	
30-second review	i-ii, 95, 152	
Volunteer experience	24	
Work experience		
Statements	4, 15-26, 49, 53	

ISBN 1412068282-2